WHAT MEN WEAR
and WHY

A publication by the makers of FANTASTIC MAN mapping the wardrobe habits of 50 very interesting men

Plus, three sprawling bonus interviews, live from the dressing rooms of designers STEFANO PILATI, CHARLES JEFFREY and PAUL SMITH

BART DE BAETS and the knitted sweater

A questionnaire from November 2016 with the Belgian-born graphic designer. Bart lives and works in the Dutch city of Amsterdam, where he also teaches at the acclaimed Gerrit Rietveld Academie.

What garment is key to your personal style?

That would have to be the knitted sweater.

How many knitted sweaters do you have in your wardrobe?

I have a large number of knitted sweaters, but because I wear them so frequently, they soon get worn out and I throw them away. None of my sweaters are spectacular or outrageous; they're all kind of moody and muddy-coloured. The colour scheme is more or less dominated by navy blues, browns and dark greens. I think I have about 20 that I wear regularly. Some of the ones that have holes are among my favourites.

What is it specifically about knitted sweaters that you love?

There's a certain kind of nerdiness to wearing and owning lots of knitted sweaters. Like a son who has lived with his parents for too long. It has something to do with the need to have a uniform, but one that can vary. The idea of the update is vital. A lot depends on what I wear underneath one of these dull sweaters. My collection is easily made more interesting when combined with T-shirts and buttoned-up shirts. Then there's the whole idea of tucking in sweaters. I kind of like that, too. Tucking in a sweater fits the nerdy stereotype, but there's also something hooligan-like about it. I like my sweaters kind of short, right up to the waist, showing a belt buckle or my wrists.

Do you know where your attachment to sweaters comes from?

When I was an art student I picked up a book from the library called 'Jong!' [Young!], which gave an overview of youth culture in the Netherlands starting in the early '60s. JOHAN VAN DER KEUKEN's pictures from 'Wij Zijn 17' [We Are 17] were featured heavily in the book. One picture showed a young black guy holding a trumpet and wearing an old, greyish-purple polo-collar sweater. He also wore skinny jeans, showing a glimpse of his socks. His shoes were plain brown. I often use the memory of that image when shopping, or when getting dressed. I have a few of these pictures that I keep in mind for the same purpose. And in a way they are all kind of similar. They represent a particular kind of plainly dressed guy. Always good-looking though.

Are you happy to have the whole world wear "your" knitted sweaters or do you prefer to stand out?

A good sweater, often an old worn one, can look really quite sexy. Wearing sweaters doesn't make me stand out. I don't expect them to make me do so.

Have you ever considered settling on a strict uniform and what would it be? Would you consider it a relief, or a loss of options?

Although I think I am quite sensitive to fashion and trends, my wardrobe or personal way of dressing has not changed drastically over the last, let's say, ten years. I would not consider it a uniform, nor would I say that I dress according to some kind of dress code. The idea of not having to think about what to wear in the morning seems attractive but wouldn't suit me. I like to think of dressing up as a way of styling myself. So, all other details – rolling up, tucking in, the socks, wearing layers – are part of the fun of it and are changing constantly. There was a strict dress code at my high school and I was often amazed by the things kids did to their clothes in order to bend the rules and to not get in trouble. That idea of dressing with certain restrictions fascinates me.

Who or what do you look at for style inspiration? Do you look at fashion?

In 2011 I spent some months in Cairo for

an artist residency, and the men there often wore oversized, short-sleeved shirts, making the short sleeves reach the elbows. I think that's a great look, with big, wide slacks buckled up to quite high. Again, it's a certain clumsiness that I appreciate. I also like how the Turkish kids in my neighbourhood wear slim-fitting ADIDAS track pants, although I wouldn't wear those myself.

Can you describe the state of your closet? Is it tidy, messy, super organised?

I recently started watching a show called 'London Spy', where one of the main characters is a manically neat categoriser. There's no chance that could ever be me. I am really into precisely folding laundry, though. I used to live with flatmates for years and they would let me fold their laundry, which I didn't mind doing while watching television.

What ultimately signifies your style of dressing?

I like the idea of myself as the stylish nerd and my outfit looking a bit hard, as if it was outlined, like in a cartoon. I roll up my trousers like any old hipster does and I casually roll up the sleeves of a sweater, just a little. I tighten my belt so that my pants are quite high up – good for the crotch and ass area. I also wear white low CONVERSE or REEBOK sneakers to look boyish or clumsy.

THOMAS CHATTERTON WILLIAMS and the V-neck T-shirt

A questionnaire from November 2018 with the American writer living in Paris. Thomas was interviewed before a game of squash.

What garment is key to your personal style?

I think the V-neck T-shirt. Throughout the years it was a white kind of traditional HANES V-neck, but as I got older I started to treat myself to specifically VINCE T-shirts. I have a kind of slim build and I'm tall and lanky and these T-shirts fit me perfectly...

How many of these T-shirts do you have in your wardrobe?

I've only just bought the third one, but I've been washing them constantly and wearing them several times a week since 2010. It's a $55 T-shirt but they've lasted. The one I'm wearing has come apart so I'm ordering new ones this month but that's eight years of wear.

What is it specifically about this garment that you love?

The practicality! I have two in navy blue and one in black. It goes with everything. I wear it under a sweater; I wear it by itself in the warm weather. You wear it with a nice watch or a nice pair of sunglasses, a pair of good jeans and some sneakers and you feel like you've got yourself an outfit.

Is the angle and depth of the V important?

Yes, the V on VINCE T-shirts is the best for me because it has a wider, shallow neck that goes well with a slimmer build. AMERICAN APPAREL brought deep, narrow, super acute Vs into the game that were down to the belly button. It was absurd. Basically, my whole life was in crew-necks until my late twenties because I have a very skinny neck and I felt like the V-neck was exposing that. But if you find the right V, what makes it better than a crewneck is that it doesn't show under a sweater. You don't have a double collar. But you don't want to take off your sweater and have your whole sternum exposed.

Where does your attachment to this T-shirt come from?

I'm a New Jersey kid, very hip-hop influenced. In the late '90s and early '00s, there was a white tee craze where everybody would be swimming in these enormous white T-shirts, and I was at the very tail end of that.

As I was transitioning into my early twenties I started to wear slimmer and slimmer versions of the white T-shirt, and then you would just buy three packs of HANES and toss them after a few wears. Eventually I was walking through Saks Fifth Avenue in San Francisco and I saw one of these VINCE T-shirts on sale. I think it was $25 and I thought that was still expensive for a T-shirt, but it's the perfect T-shirt. It's soft. It feels well made.

Have you tried out other brands of V-neck?

I've been given several SUNSPEL T-shirts that are even more expensive, and supposedly they compete with VINCE, but I don't know. They don't fit right. The slim ones are a little too short; there's something not quite right.

How do you feel when you see other men wearing this garment?

The only other man I've seen wearing these specific T-shirts is my brother because I started giving them to him, and then he started buying his own. I want my brother to feel as good in his T-shirts as I do!

There are lots of Americans in Paris. Do you think there is a Parisian-American way of dressing?

When Americans come here they immediately start learning to wear scarves. A European man can tie a scarf in ways that few Americans will.

Do you have a dress code for work?

I have to fight against doing my work in my underwear or pyjamas or bathrobe. I try to get dressed for the day as though I'm going to meet with someone even though I'm not. I force myself to go to cafes. I've noticed the way you look, the way you present yourself to the world subtly influences the thoughts that go through your head. If you put on a blazer and sit down at a table, you write a little bit differently than if you are walking around in your sweatpants.

What do you wear to look sexy?

My wife recently gave me an HERMÈS carré: a cashmere and silk scarf. You can't tell me I'm not sexy when I'm wearing it. I don't know if I actually am, but I feel sexy.

STEPHEN JONES and the hat

A questionnaire from January 2017 with the 59-year-old milliner and nightlife legend. Stephen is originally from West Kirby, UK, but has lived in London since the '70s.

What garment is key to your personal style?

A hat!

How many do you have in your wardrobe?

In my personal wardrobe, I probably have about 100.

What is it about hats that you love?

They are completely transformative.

What are the defining specifications that make the perfect hat?

If I'm in England and working from home then it can be quite varied, but if I'm travelling, which I do for maybe half the year, it needs to be packable in my LOUIS VUITTON hat box.

Are you happy to have the whole world wear "your" garment?

I am happy for the world to wear the same hat as me. For example, when I see my friends CHRIS SULLIVAN or CHRISTOS and we're all wearing berets, we always laugh and say, "Oh! The beret boys!"

Who or what do you look at for style inspiration? Do you look at fashion?

I don't know, it depends on the season really. In autumn or winter, I think of TERRY THOMAS in his hilarious tweeds and bowler hats. In spring, I think of Count ROBERT DE MONTESQUIOU. His portrait by GIOVANNI BOLDINI has always been an extraordinary inspiration. For a summer party it always has to be DONALD SUTHERLAND in 'Casanova': pink ruffles! Do I look at fashion?

Well, yes, of course I do. As RuPAUL said, "We're all born naked and the rest is drag."

Can you describe the state of your closet? Is it tidy, or messy?

My closet is actually quite small, but it is tidy because it has to be. I have boxes for special shoes, but normal shoes just get thrown around. My hats are organised by delicacy. For example, my handmade straw boater is in its own hat box, my THOM BROWNE bowler is in another hat box filled with caps, and my berets from Japan are actually in a FORTNUM & MASON's hamper.

Is there a garment that you used to dislike but ended up loving and wearing?

Yes, I very much disliked polo shirts because they absolutely did not suit me, but now my long-sleeved FRED PERRY polo shirts are a staple of my wardrobe. I've got one in every colour, and I wish they would produce more colours so I could buy more! What changed my mind? I lost 38 kilos.

Have you ever considered settling on a strict uniform and if so, what would it be? Would you consider it a relief?

Funnily enough, I do wear a bit of a uniform. I like wearing a suit because, in a way, it can do the work for you. You don't always have to sit with perfect posture, with shoulders back and a straight leg, because that's what a suit looks like. So a semi-constructed suit is a fantastic uniform and it means you can accessorise in many different ways.

Do you have a dress code for work?

When I am selling couture hats, I do need to be dressed appropriately.

What do you wear to look sexy? Do you have a pick-up look?

I don't, but when I have picked-up, I have often been wearing shorts, by chance.

What defines your style of dressing?

Well, the easy answer is a hat, and that's what people expect from me. I've always been interested in looking older than I am, and never younger than I am, because I think it gives me an authority I otherwise do not have.

IAN BRADLEY and the denim jacket

A questionnaire from March 2017 with a New York City stylist. Ian was born in Ohio, the seventh most populous state in the US.

What garment is key to your personal style?

A denim jacket.

How many denim jackets do you have in your wardrobe?

Six.

What is it specifically about denim jackets that you love?

They can add a personal touch and a casual attitude to any outfit.

What are the defining specifications of the perfect denim jacket?

I like them to be snug, almost too small.

Do you know where your attachment to denim jackets comes from? Is it something from your youth, or something you picked up from a specific person?

I associated them with cool kids when I was young and that was reinforced in my teenage years by people like KATE MOSS, THE STROKES and LAURYN HILL. They always seemed cool without pretension.

Are you happy to have the whole world wear "your" garment or do you much prefer to stand out?

I'm happy to see anyone wear a denim jacket since it's a garment that works on everyone. I really love seeing older men wearing denim jackets they've clearly have had for many years.

Can you describe the state of your closet? Is it tidy, messy, super organised?

It's all of the above! A bit messy, things are kinda organised, folded, and yet there are still piles of clothing. There's clothing in every nook and cranny of my room.

Is there a garment that you used to dislike

but ended up loving and wearing? What changed your mind?

Sweatpants. Always loathed them growing up; thought they looked lazy. But I was given a pair about four years ago and ended up wearing them all the time. I guess I've just succumbed to the athleisure trend.

Have you ever made a radical change in your "look"?

The last radical thing I did was bleach my hair two years ago. Never again.

Have you ever considered settling on a strict uniform and if so, what would it be? Would you consider it a welcome relief, or a loss of options?

I romanticise the idea of uniform dressing, but don't think I'll ever get there. I would get bored too quickly.

What do you wear to look sexy? Do you have a pick up look?

A T-shirt tucked into well-fitting trousers to accentuate the bum and waist.

What amazing tip for wardrobe management or maintenance can you share?

I'm not the one to give advice for this, but I'm open to any guidance.

RICHARD GRAY and the cagoule

A questionnaire from July 2018 with the 46-year-old British fashion writer. Richard was interviewed on a sunny morning in London's Golden Square.

What garment is key to your personal style?

The cagoule. It is just a really brilliantly odd, dynamic piece of apparel. It has some really weird connotations; there is a certain nerdiness to it and I really enjoy how awkward it is. If it walked into a room at a party it would stand on its own – it's nobody's friend, it's a loner garment.

Just for the sake of clarity, what do you mean when you say cagoule?

A waterproof, showerproof over garment in a bright colour. I'll accept a zip-through thing but a pullover is definitely my favourite.

Materials?

Anything starting with "Poly". It has got to be man-made; that's the new luxury.

Exactly how many cagoules do you have in your wardrobe?

I reckon I've collected 17 or so. I originally lost my cagoule hymen to a COMME DES GARÇONS SHIRT one, which I still have. It's a brilliant navy colour with a plastic thing on the front which has some indecipherable words on it. Everyone stares at it which I really like: a cagoule is odd anyway, so when you find an oddly designed cagoule, that's even better. It's odd in the extreme.

What are the defining specifications that make the perfect cagoule?

It needs a drawstring hood to up the nerd quotient whilst keeping the rain out, a drawstring waist is also really nice. You can pull it up and tie it higher so it balloons a bit. It also looks best when it is creased from being in your rucksack or tied around your chest.

Do you know where your attachment to this garment comes from? Is it something from your youth? Because it is quite a childish garment.

I've seen pictures of my brothers and me when we were younger and I'm always the one in the cagoule so I do think these things stick with you. I blame my mother, although I blame her for many things...

How do you feel when you see other men wearing the same thing? Are you happy to have the whole world to wear "your" garment or do you prefer to stand out?

When I see men in cagoules I feel as if they are pissing on my fashion lamppost.

People should steer clear of your territory?

Yes. I'm particularly bothered by a recent wave of Northern European cagoule-alikes, the cagoule-erati. Back off OUR LEGACY.

Have you ever made a radical change in your look? Would you be tempted to start again from scratch?

Every year I fantasise about just getting rid of everything and spending the rest of my life in MARGARET HOWELL. But that is only because I want to subscribe to the lifestyle of someone who only wears MARGARET HOWELL: an art director or someone that visits galleries every weekend instead of just waking up hung-over on Sunday.

Would that be your uniform? Or what would your ideal uniform be?

I'd have a room with 100 white shirts by AGNÈS B., 100 COMME DES GARÇONS HOMME DEUX trousers in navy and ADIDAS Stan Smith trainers, all in a line. I'd just go and stand next to them and sniff them. It would be so freeing – you could then concentrate on the important things, because fashion is so peripheral. Fashion is fucking hard at my age; it's hard to be a part of it but not become a victim. I think there is something really, really cool about discipline.

Do you have a dress code for work? Does your work influence what you wear?

Anyone who works in fashion and says they don't turn it up for the shows is lying. Everyone does, and if they don't, they are still making an equally as considered decision as those that do. I went to Pitti Uomo and I just wanted to set fire to the whole thing; there's so much forced hetero posturing! It's this circus of shape-throwing guys in tartan three-piece suits. But it is not necessarily the posers that are the evil – it's the lazy press who take pictures of them. That freaky, costume-like way of dressing has become a byword for the fashion industry. It's not fashion; it's just middle-aged men trying to out-suit each other.

What amazing tip for wardrobe management or maintenance can you share?

I love DYLON machine dye – if you could snort it, I would. The black dye should be an investment for everybody. Just make sure you clean your tub out properly afterwards because it really gets in everywhere. I spend so much money on UNDERCOVER T-shirts, and if I'm going to spend that much then I'm going to re-dye them.

KAMAL AHMED and his television suit

A questionnaire from October 2018 with the economics editor of the BBC. Now editorial director of the British broadcaster, Kamal was interviewed in a glass-walled room at their London headquarters.

What garment is key to your personal style?

I think that would have to be my suit.

Just the one suit?

I've got three or four which are all lovely, but I've got one which is kind of my game suit – if I know I have a particularly important interview or big day I will plan to make sure I hit my top suit on that day.

What does your game suit look like?

It has changed a bit. I'm a bit more sober in how I dress now, so my palette is mainly navy or grey. My game suit at the moment is a navy light flannel single-button suit, made by a British tailor called MARC WALLACE. I'd probably wear that with a MARGARET HOWELL tie. If I'm interviewing the governor of the Bank of England, that's the suit.

Pardon my ignorance but, as economics editor of the BBC, how often are you actually on television? Is your job quite public facing or are you more behind the scenes?

I'm on air a lot: two to three times a week. Then there's radio and online, but yeah, I'm on telly pretty regularly.

What's the logic behind what people wear on television?

The key to style on television is wearing things that you don't notice – that's almost the point. I don't want whatever I'm wearing to be the thing that people are thinking about when they look at me. You want them to be listening to what you're saying or looking at what you're doing.

But as a media personality surely you don't want to be anonymous?

No... when you go into television you do think, "Am I going to have a thing? Is there a thing that visually identifies me?" – like JON SNOW's ties or NICK ROBINSON's glasses. I thought a very well-cut suit might be my thing, and I do have a bit of a reputation for suits now, but you don't want to be distracting. You should always dress a bit more sober on television. It took me a little while to learn that when I first started at the BBC.

Are there any rules about what you can and can't wear? Don't stripes cause problems?

Yes, stripes create a strobe effect, so you should wear plain colours in blocks. But there aren't many rules really – you wear a suit partly because it's a utilitarian thing; it's a uniform and it won't get in the way of a story. If you are wearing a load of random stuff...

It's distracting.

Yes.

And not necessarily distracting in an eye-catching sense; it's distracting because it's incongruous. We are just so used to seeing men on the news wearing suits.

Exactly that. Which raises an interesting question. You don't want to be distracting, but as new audiences develop, younger generations start watching, maybe we could rethink how we look and feel on air. Maybe we don't always need to be in suits. Because there's the other side of wearing a suit – if it's not done right it can feel top-down: "I'm telling you things, sit up and listen." Maybe you want to break down some of those barriers, I don't know.

Surely you must be thinking about these things more and more often, as a suit doesn't necessarily still reflect the reality of how men dress.

I suppose the big thing for us is, "What do our audiences expect?" The old cliché is that the news, even on the radio, would be read in a dinner suit, and it was. You had to be serious, and seriousness was equated with a dinner suit. We've moved on from there, but there's an expectation from our audience that we should be suitably attired, and that might be a suit and tie. You're right, in lots of professions and sectors people have moved away from wearing suits, but it comes down to the particular audience. I'm the economics editor of the BBC, so I think, broadly, my audience would expect me to wear a suit. If I turned up in jeans, trainers and a T-shirt it would just send the wrong kind of message. It doesn't mean that nobody can; it just means that I'm not going to be first to start dressing down.

Do you dress a certain way depending on how you are going to be seen on camera? If you know you are going to be presenting from behind a desk, do you not worry so much about your shoes?

I'm rarely behind a desk, but I'm often out and about or I'm interviewing somebody, and I do think about it, yeah. If I know I'm doing an interview I might give my shoes a quick polish because I know you will see them, especially if I'm doing what's called "walking", where sometimes there's just a tight shot of your shoes as you are walking past. You don't want your dirty shoes on the TV. There have been times when I've had a hole in the shoe and it has shown. It looks like you're not really taking it seriously.

Have you always worn suits or is it something you started doing for television?

I've always worn them. I turned up on my first day of work in a three-piece suit. It was a small local paper just outside Glasgow.

You wore them as a child?

Actually, no I didn't. I'm not quite like JACOB REES-MOGG. I don't know what it was. I always liked nice clothes and then suddenly I had a tiny bit of money. I mean tiny, but I would genuinely save up my money to buy nice suits. I would forecast my suits over a number of years and figure out when I could buy the next one. I was really into NICOLE FARHI, and her suits were expensive!

You are rather tall.

I am.

How tall are you, if you don't mind?

Six foot four.

Do you dress to emphasise your height?

I'm lucky that I am slim rather than tall – I have a reasonable silhouette. I think that quite trim cuts suit me because of my shape. I am aware of that and I try and dress accordingly. I don't look great in baggy clothes. I buy most things, T-shirts for example, in small, which is quite unusual; shop assistants always tell me I'll never fit a small.

On the weekends are you still in suits or do you dress more casually?

Oh no, I dress more casually, I really do enjoy wearing more casual clothes. I shop a bit at ACNE. I go to DOVER STREET MARKET, MARGARET HOWELL, SUNSPEL. I quite like TOAST. I try to avoid that awkward look which is the middle-aged man in jeans and a white shirt on the weekend.

That is very sensible of you.

It's a bad look!

DANIEL HAWORTH and his double-pleated woollen trousers

A questionnaire from October 2016 with a 22-year-old Savile Row tailor. Now slightly older, Daniel still works on Savile Row and is director of the house Maurice Sedwell.

What garment is key to your personal style?

Double-pleated woollen trousers.

How many double-pleated woollen trousers do you have in your wardrobe?

Five.

What is it specifically about these kinds of trousers that you love?

They're extremely versatile. A slim-legged dark pair can be worn with a matching suit or with a plain T-shirt and trainers. I've also made pairs that I have cut with a much wider leg, and again they can look smart or casual depending on what you wear them with. I also find the look of the two pleats at the front of the trouser very elegant. The front pleat runs into the crease and the second is there to bear the weight of the first so it hangs straight down the leg.

Do you know where your attachment to the double pleat comes from?

My affinity for the double-pleated trouser comes from my interest in how clothing and fashion have changed over time. It is such a staple piece and comes up time and time again in different cuts, lengths and styles. I used to think that they looked a bit old fashioned, but after making a pair for myself and seeing the silhouette they create, I was quickly won over and have made several since.

How do you feel when you see other men wearing the same things as you?

All my clothes feel personal to me, as I've made a lot of them by hand and there's a lot of labour that has gone into each item. I'm not too fussed with what other people wear, but if the whole world dressed like me, it would be a very boring place.

Who or what do you look at for style inspiration? Do you look at fashion?

London is a big influence on how I dress. It's a city with such a rich history of dressing, and I think growing up here you are very aware of it: Mods, Teddy Boys, football casuals, East End dockers, '60s West End peacocks. When I was growing up, the garage and grime scene in London was in its prime and highly influential in the way that I thought about dressing and clothes. You needed the right tracksuit (AKADEMIKS, ECKO UNLIMITED or a grey marl baggy NIKE tracksuit), the right NEW ERA hat (I had an LA Lakers one) and the right NIKE bag (the small 'Just Do It' bags). It even came down to having the correct mobile phone (a MOTOROLA RAZR or the square NOKIA 7600). I take inspiration and little bits from all of these groups as influence on how I dress.

Can you describe the state of your closet? Is it tidy, messy, super organised?

My room is a mess. It's just piles of clothes. However, I'm good with an iron, so it's no problem.

Is there a garment that you used to dislike but ended up loving and wearing?

One of the first pairs of trousers I made for myself was a pair of silver-grey mohair trousers with a very faint blue stripe. One pleat. They were made of a very unusual cloth and I found it very difficult to wear them with anything as it was really a suiting cloth. However, I found that they looked great with a white T-shirt and CONVERSE and I wear them all the time now. Also mohair is a cloth that, once pressed, looks really sharp. It holds its crease really well. I like the contrast between this and the more casual elements like CONVERSE or a grey hoodie.

Have you ever considered settling on a strict uniform, and if so, what would it be?

I've always found that idea incredibly boring. I find dressing and wearing different clothes too much fun.

Do you have a dress code for work?

As a bespoke tailor, I wear my handmade suits to work. I like suits that really highlight the possibilities of tailoring: strong, sculpted shoulder lines, shaping out the chest with hand-padded canvas so that you can show off a smaller waist. I prefer a high-waisted trouser as it creates a long, slim leg.

Do you have a pick-up look?

I don't think I have ever consciously worn anything because I thought someone would find it attractive. I just wear what I like and feel confident in.

What amazing tip for wardrobe management can you share?

I try to wash my clothes as little as possible (underwear aside of course). Washing damages the cloth and fades the colours, especially on the finer fabrics I make many of my clothes from. Hanging items and letting them air would be my best tip.

What is it that ultimately signifies your style of dressing?

I like clothing that's quite classic or symbolic – from the suits that I wear to work and the penny loafers I wear with them to the raw denim jeans with REEBOK classics and a trench coat I wear to go to the pub. They all feel like staple items of clothing. I don't like to wear clothes that are heavily branded.

IRVIN PASCAL and the Breton-striped T-shirt

A questionnaire from June 2018 with the visual artist. In his previous career, Irvin was a professional boxer.

What garment is key to your personal style?

I've pretty much become a Breton-striped T-shirt collector.

How many Breton-striped T-shirts do you have in your wardrobe?

Probably around 30.

Are they all classic navy-and-blue ones?

No, I've got lots of variations. Although thinking about it, a lot of them are just different versions of the same T-shirt. I have them in different colours, some have thicker stripes, different materials, there are unlimited options with the Breton T-shirt. My go-to one is predominantly white with bold black stripes.

Do you know where your attachment to the Breton T-shirt comes from?

I think my love of the style came from PICASSO and WARHOL; they were big fans. It's sparked a broader interest in the history of stripes. Even the ancient Egyptians were wearing stripes...

Ancient Egyptians?

Yeah, if you look at the death mask of TUTANKHAMUN it has stripes on it! I think the Breton stripe emerged in the French navy. It was worn by French sailors in order to make it easier for them to be seen amongst the waves. I guess that is still true today as you can see someone wearing one so easily in a crowded street; it's so distinctive.

What is it specifically about the Breton stripe that you love? (continued on p. 18)

Live from STEFANO PILATI's wardrobe

From his sprawling labyrinth of a dressing room speaks the Italian designer who started his career as an intern at Cerruti, assisted Armani, Prada and Tom Ford and then rose to the heady fashion peaks of directing Yves Saint Laurent for almost eight years and Ermenegildo Zegna for three. Stefano lives in Berlin, with his work-space upstairs, his palatial apartment and matching walk-in one floor below. His incredible archive of super personal garments now serves as the inspiration for Random Identities, the label he has just launched. Interview by GERT JONKERS.

Before we enter the sacred grounds of your wardrobe, can you tell me how this closet-slash-archive came about?

It wasn't until I moved to Berlin six years ago that I first began living and working in the same space. I'd never had that in Paris or Milan, and I'd never even thought of doing it, but once I had this opportunity I just realised how much I need these clothes around me, and how much more rewarding my work can be in the proximity of my wardrobe. All of a sudden, I realised that my wardrobe – the dimensions of my wardrobe, the archive of everything I've collected – is of huge value to my work. I have an enormous amount of clothing, and a good percentage of that is what I designed or bought with the allowances I had when I was at PRADA, ARMANI or wherever.

Where did you keep it all before Berlin? Was it in storage somewhere outside of Paris?

Some was in storage, yes, and some was in trunks in my basement in Paris. Already in Milan I had a pretty good wardrobe because I never threw anything away, really. Some things I lost, and some things maybe my mother threw away. Like, when you're in your twenties and you're, like, "Where's that shirt that I left here?" And your mother says, "I threw it away."

The horror!

"Mother, what do you mean?!" So yes, now I really enjoy having my whole wardrobe at hand when I'm making something and I think of a collar that was perfect, or a lapel that was perfect. Now I can just get it from my wardrobe and reapply it. The relevance of my wardrobe has become more important to me than ever. It has become my heritage. Do you see what I'm saying?

Totally.

And I think that links to the launch of my brand. That's what RANDOM IDENTITIES is: it's my wardrobe. I design the stuff that I don't have or can't find, or that I have but want to refine – a puzzle that combines the classic and the perennial, where design becomes a mix of memory and tradition and innovation, legacy, everything.

Shall we explore your wardrobe? I can't wait.

Yes. But darling, do you mind if I ask you to take off your shoes?

Not at all. [Opens the door to a giant room full of mirror-door closets] Oh, wow!

I'm a bit shy about this... It's very personal.

I was thinking about how getting dressed is a very vulnerable act, and how I never like it when my boyfriend or anybody watches me while I get dressed, while I try things on in front of a mirror. I don't mind being naked in front anybody, but I dread getting dressed with somebody around. Do you have that?

I'm fine with CHRIS or friends being around when I get dressed. What I hate is packing. I need to be alone when I pack. I have it more than ever now that I live in Berlin. Here you can wear whatever. Berlin doesn't require any formality and that has changed the way I dress. So every time I go to New York or London or Paris or whatever, I almost feel like it's an event, and I'm, like, "What am I wearing?"

Just to be clear for the readers, I'll describe what you're wearing now: baggy white cotton trousers with paint stains on them that I think are from your YVES SAINT LAURENT "Painter" collection from Spring and Summer 2008.

No, these are the original trousers. These are the ones I bought from a painter that was painting at the Beaubourg.

What was he painting?

He was painting the room at the Beaubourg all pink for the womenswear show.

And you bought the pants off him right there?

Yes, because I really liked them, and then I did the menswear collection based on them. I didn't keep much from that collection – maybe the shoes, maybe a suit. But these trousers I wear all the time.

I still have a T-shirt from that collection, with the YSL logo painted on it.

Oh, that's cute.

You're wearing your trousers with a shocking-pink cotton belt.

This I bought from the surplus store. I liked that they had so many colours and you just buy them at the counter. I'm wearing it for the first time.

Okay. And your stripy socks?

I bought them at the market here. They're a bit felted. This sweatshirt is my original 1950s sweatshirt, and I wear a T-shirt from JAMES PERSE.

Do you get dressed quickly or does it take you an hour?

Very quickly. Five minutes.

Do you always enter this room with a preconceived idea? Do you know if it's going to be a light look, a casual look?

Yes, I do have an idea. Why don't you take a seat? Shall I get drinks? Do you want to see the inside of my cupboards?

Oh yes, please give me the grand tour. [Stefano swings open some of the mirrored doors] Ah, so all your knitwear goes in separate plastic bags. And everything's quite colour-coded. What's the hardware? Is it IKEA?

Yes, absolutely.

My boyfriend still hates the fact that I pushed for custom-built and very un-flexible closets at our home. He just wanted the IKEA system.

That was my reflex too. Years ago, when I bought my house in Paris, I had this beautiful wardrobe made. The insides were GIO PONTI, restored, with velvet padding on the doors. Beautiful, but when I moved here, I thought, "I need lots more space. I want cupboards that will accommodate everything," and I was trying to plan it all: hanging clothes here, drawers there, shelves, shoe racks. There was no way that I could plan all that in advance, so I just rationalised it and went to IKEA, and it's perfect!

Please show me some more.

Here are the feathers and shearlings and furs. Here are the blouson jackets. Some trench coats. Here are my gloves.

Let me report: how many gloves are there in this drawer? 40 pairs?

I don't know. I lose them all the time.

What are these funny ones made of?

That's seal.

Seal?

Seal's magnificent. Beautiful. There was this little store in SoHo, New York, called Alaska something, where you could buy Inuit products including seal. It came with a list of certificates that told you how it was made and that they were dealing with an over-population of seals since they've been protected. I bought those and a little gilet because I love seal. When I was a kid, in the '70s, we had after-ski boots in seal – back when we all thought that fur was great.

This is so spectacular. How many metres of closet doors do you have, do you know?

I don't, darling.

Let me measure. One, two, three, four, five... Ten metres. Same on the other side, that's 20. Plus an alley over here, 35. I'd say 40 metres total. Doubled, since you have a storey on top. 80 metres of wardrobe! Do you have an assistant to keep it orderly and neat?

Not really. We have a housekeeper.

Does she put the clothes back when you've dropped them on the floor?

I don't drop clothes on the floor, I actually put them back myself! If you design clothes, it's difficult to throw them on the floor. Very difficult.

That makes sense. Have you seen any other men's wardrobes as grand as yours?

Frankly, no. Well, I guess FABIO has a good wardrobe, and I imagine MARC must also have a good wardrobe.

JACOBS? Yes, MARC probably needs a whole section of his wardrobe specially for that one enormous BALENCIAGA coat he's been flaunting on Instagram.

I don't know if KARL has a big one. JOHN has a big wardrobe, I'm sure.

GALLIANO? I'm sure. Are your shoes here too?

Some are here. [Opens more doors]

I guess you don't have any strict rules for getting rid of things, like, if you've not worn something for two years, out it goes.

Oh no. This is already the essence of the essence.

Who polishes your leather boots? They're beaming!

My housekeeper does that. But I can do better! Look at these PRADA boots from the '90s. [Points to a pair of green nylon ankle boots with a red stripe on the heel] I saw some kids in London wearing them recently, in black, and I was like, shit, I have those in green but I wish I had them in black; I would wear them more often.

Why don't you have a look on eBay to see if you can find them?

Second-hand shoes? Oh no, never! Look, these PRADA's are from when I was working there. [Holds up a pair of slender, low, square-toed lace-ups with a sporty sole] Divine! These shoes are divine for what they were, especially at that time. This was pre-PRADA SPORT. Imagine the influence that this shoe last had on the shoes of today.

Do you still wear these or would you wait a few more years?

I don't know... You know what, I'm not that silhouette anymore – let's put it that way. My shoes have changed more than anything else. I can't wear elegant, light shoes anymore. I have difficulty with shoes in the summer. Trainers are good, of course, but what else? The worst is evening shoes. When you really need to wear something chic and you can't wear sneakers. I guess you could wear loafers.

You've just made some great very-high-heeled boots for RANDOM IDENTITIES that I think are perfect for you for evenings.

Well, yes, absolutely. See, here they are. They were an experiment. I had to wear them myself because, as I said, everything I do, I do for myself. I try things, and at some point I give them to others to wear and see what they think.

Is that how the RANDOM IDENTITIES collection came together?

What I presented isn't a collection.

It's not a collection?

No, these are a few items put together. Do you see what I mean? I don't know how to say it differently. It may look like a collection because I presented it as a collection, in the format of a fashion show [in Montreal on 7 November 2018]. Call it whatever, but to me it's not really a collection, nor was this a show. It's funny how if you put some garments out there as a sequence, and you show them with a walk involved, suddenly it's perceived as a collection, and as a catwalk show – and even as my comeback!

But that's not how you see it?

No. A comeback from what? I never went away as far as I'm concerned. And what I just showed are clothes that work for me, that fit me right now, or would fit me on an imaginary occasion, or would have fit me had I been ten years younger, or that I already had but just made a little bit more precious. And it's something that could only happen because I was working in this proximity to my wardrobe.

I see...

Are you bored, my GERT?

No no, I'm thinking.

Tell me what you're thinking.

I'm thinking about how your collection is not a collection. Which I find interesting. Indeed, why would one call it a "collection"? Or why would we apply a brand model to whatever you feel like doing?

I have plans, of course; otherwise I wouldn't have started. It took me two years to put this together, but my plan is to structure it around what I really need. It's not money or glory. It's pure passion. And I can't live without fashion, obviously. You can see that in my wardrobe. It may have taken me 50 years to figure it out, but now I know: I cannot live without fashion.

That's clear, yes. You'd be heartbroken if your wardrobe were taken away from you, wouldn't you?

Are you kidding? Of course! The one thing I still beg for is clothes. If I saw something on you that I really loved, I'd get really irritated, jealous, envious. I'm not kidding. I'd make sure that I got it off of you.

Do you do that? Do you talk people out of their clothes on the spot?

If I want it, I try to get it, yes.

I used to do that ages ago. When I'd be in a club and I'd see somebody wearing a T-shirt that I liked, I'd go up to them and propose to swap shirts, and quite often they'd say yes.

Really? With a stranger? That's good! I've never done that.

Well, you did it with the painter who was wearing your trousers.

I bought them. I gave him €100. That's different. But if it were a friend of mine, I would just beg them until I got it.

I think that's great.

I don't know if it's great or not; I just can't help it. It's like saying that I'm blond. I don't know if that's good or bad. It is what it is.

Speaking of your hair, I love your haircut. I was just talking to my hairdresser about mullets and here you are with an amazing mullet.

Do you like it? Thank you for saying so. A mullet with curly hair like mine is basically 99 per cent of the time a disaster.

Well, I think you found that magical one per cent.

I'm glad you like it. CHRISTIAAN cut my hair. He scared the shit out of me.

Since you say you've rarely thrown anything out, what do you think is the oldest garment you have in your wardrobe? Do you still have shirts from when you were a kid?

I was just thinking about that. I have some bandanas that are really old. Like, really old. I started wearing those bloody bandanas when I was, like, 14. And I still have a FIORUCCI jacket that I bought when I was 17, so that must have been 1982. And pants. I have so many pants. Pants are fabulous. Pants give you everything.

If you have one absolute favourite type of garment, would it be pants?

Well, darling, we're men! If we don't love pants, we're fucked. Pants are like skirts for women. Pants are movement, proportion... If you're a man and you don't love pants or don't know how to wear pants, what are you going to do? I love pants.

How do you store your pants? Is there a special system?

I'll show you. [Opens door]

Okay, so mostly hanging, some lying. God, it's amazing to see these rows and rows of trousers in every possible shade of grey and realise what the human mind is able to store and process, because you probably know every trouser hanging there and can deal with that information in a split second.

I know. For me, everything is work-related. This wardrobe is not some narcissistic treasure. It's not like I stare at these clothes in doubt, wondering what to wear. If that were the case, it would take me three hours to get dressed... If you have a collection like this, you need to know how to handle it, and you do it because it's your joy. And you learn how to take care of your clothes. It's what I said earlier: I can't throw my clothes on the floor because all this has been designed, made, earned or bought, and I find it disrespectful to be nonchalant about that.

Respect your clothes, yes.

Well, I wouldn't be a designer otherwise, would I? Why are my shoes kept so well polished? Because there's nothing that I hate more than dirty shoes. Unless they're shoes that are sexy when they are dirty. But that rarely happens.

Are you ever temped to go back to designing for a big house?

With my mind, sure. With my gut, no way.

Because there must have been brands like LANVIN or CELINE or BURBERRY knocking on your door in recent years?

Absolutely not. They know that I'm the most difficult designer in fashion.

Difficult in what sense?

I don't know. Ask around. I'm so difficult that it's obviously difficult to avoid it. It took me a while to realise that I'm happy being difficult, because I know so much and I know exactly how things work because I did them in the past. I know I'm difficult for the people around me, but how can I not be? You need to be on top of things to make them your own. Otherwise it's a compromise.

(Ends)

(continued from p. 11) It belongs to all people. It has been worn by all classes: from the Parisian bourgeoisie to normal working-class people today. No one owns the look, and it's interesting to see how different people bring different styles to it.

Where do you see your collection going? Will you ever have too many?

I don't think so, or at least I hope not. It would be annoying if I woke up one day and decided I hated them. I've started to take special care of the older ones to try and preserve them for as long as possible; I hardly wear the first one I ever bought for fear of damaging it.

Aside from TUTANKHAMUN, who or what do you look at for style inspiration? Do you look at fashion?

Growing up in London I was really into grime music and streetwear, and I still look at music videos to see what the flavours are these days in that scene. I look at fashion magazines, too, but I don't like to immerse myself too much in that world.

Is there a garment that you used to dislike but ended up loving and wearing? When did your aversion to it turn to fondness? What changed your mind?

When I was younger I used to hate wearing shiny shoes. My mum would make me wear them to church and I found them so disturbing, but now I'm actually starting to embrace them.

Do you have a dress code for work? Does your work influence what you wear?

Of course it does. When you are around people in a similar industry to yourself their fashion sense rubs off on you. It might be more obvious in the business world where everyone wears a suit, but the same thing exists in the art world, where a kind of informal dress code or common style is definitely present. When I'm in the studio I'm covered in paint and dirt with appalling trainers, but I always try and polish up a bit when I'm showing my work or in galleries. I used to be a professional boxer – there, your body kind of becomes your work uniform rather than the clothes you put over it.

That's so true, although it's pretty much the only sport where you get to choose what you wear while doing it.

Yeah, it's interesting to see what people choose. When ANTHONY JOSHUA walks out in his white robes he looks like a deity... like an angel! It's a very iconic image.

Do you still do any boxing?

No, I stopped about five or six years ago. But I do still hold the record for the fastest knockout in British amateur boxing history.

Wow!

DMITRY KOMIS and the bow tie

A questionnaire from October 2016 with a gallery director from New York City. Dmitry helms the David Lewis gallery, located at 88 Eldridge Street.

What garment is key to your personal style?

Bow ties. Although the occasions when I would wear bow ties are rather limited and specific, they are indispensable to my wardrobe and define my personal (evening) style.

How many different bow ties do you have in your wardrobe?

A hundred plus. I'm a compulsive collector – okay, hoarder. I don't wear all of them, I rotate probably 10 to 15 regularly. I have some amazing one-of-a-kind and vintage pieces from various eras and cultures that would probably look too costume-y if I tried to wear them.

What is it specifically about bow ties that you love?

I've always liked accessories that accentuate the neck: scarves, ties, bow ties, etcetera. I used to collect neck ties in my early twenties, I had probably close to 500 ties.

Then I stopped wearing ties altogether and moved on to scarves and bow ties. I think a big part of the interest also came from studying art history, and specifically military and aristocratic portraits throughout the centuries. I think I was more interested in how these dead men looked than I was in how most men of my generation looked.

How do you feel when you see other men wearing bow ties? Are you happy to have the whole world wear them or do you prefer to stand out?

I like to think it's my thing. I sort of hate when other men wear bow ties, unless they wear them well and at appropriate events, which rarely happens. I think most men today look pretty awful in bow ties and should never wear them. There's definitely a right and wrong way and a specific time and place to wear a bow tie. It's not like wearing a tie, which is more versatile and democratic. You should not wear a bow tie at 10am on your way to get coffee. There are some pundits (TUCKER CARLSON, GEORGE WILL, LOUIS FARRAKHAN, among others) who wear them. It's a confused, militant look. I also hate when men wear bow ties for comic effect, or paired with shorts, like they're too self-conscious to commit to the look, or it's a bizarre little-boy cutesy thing that's gross (PEE-WEE HERMAN or CHIPPENDALES). No one wore a bow tie better than KARL MARX or WINSTON CHURCHILL, except maybe JAMES BOND.

Do you know where your attachment to bow ties comes from? Is it something from your youth, or something you picked up from a specific person?

It's definitely not about youth in my case, but it is probably in some way a reaction against my generation's obsession with casual sportswear and normcore. I feel, like, men my age and younger think dressing is a chore. I definitely feel more comfortable in black tie than in gym clothes. It's also a reaction against my upbringing in the Soviet Union, where nice clothes were considered too extravagant and superfluous. You were supposed to blend in through clothes, not stand out, and men especially were not supposed to care about how they dressed.

Can you describe the state of your closet? Is it tidy, messy, super organised and are your clothes folded, boxed, grouped by colour or season, etcetera?

It's very organised, down to the uniform mahogany hangers. My husband and I have a dressing room with separate wardrobes for shirts, blazers, pants, etcetera. I have a separate closet for white shirts. Everything is rotated seasonally and accessories (sunglasses, belts, bow ties, scarves, hats, bags) are all separated accordingly in drawers and boxes. There is also a separate wardrobe for eveningwear, a closet for winter coats and a separate shoe closet.

Is there a garment that you used to dislike but ended up loving and wearing?

Denim. I used to hate it as a "democratic" fabric that was destroying the environment – it was too ridiculous. I've since eased up and embraced it, probably because I used to hate it so much. Same with fur. Growing up in Russia, I really hated seeing fur after I left; I didn't understand why people would wear it if they didn't have to. I guess everything that I now like started from some form of aversion.

Have you ever considered settling on a strict uniform and if so, what would it be?

It's not for me. I wore a uniform in school, so I equate it with children and prisons. In the art world there's already an unspoken "art fair uniform" among male dealers: dark blue denim, white shirt, navy blazer, white sneakers. Pretty exciting, isn't it? I try to steer away from that, unless I'm doing it on purpose.

Does your work influence what you wear?

I definitely dress more conservatively for work, even though the gallery atmosphere is very relaxed and not corporate. I have to travel and interact with a lot of different people regularly, and it's all about them, not me, so I don't want the focus to be on my look. I tend to save all the fun looks for my off-time.

What do you wear to look sexy? Do you have a pick-up look?

My DRIES VAN NOTEN silk suits. I don't know if they look sexy, but they definitely feel sexy. I feel sexier in long flowy silky things these days. It's not about showing skin. I used to wear a lot of tailored short shorts in my twenties, but sleeveless is probably as "sexy" as I get now. If I'm going out dancing, maybe a mesh T-shirt.

Who do you talk to when you want to talk about clothes?

The husband. Most of my friends don't really care, and honestly I'd rather talk about something else.

What amazing tip for wardrobe management or maintenance can you share?

Hand-washing or dry cleaning immediately after wearing something is incredibly important, or the oils will destroy your clothes over time, especially in between seasons. I don't think I've ever ruined any clothes in 20 years; I still wear shirts that I had in high school.

WILL SELF and the tweed jacket

A questionnaire from September 2018 with the novelist and journalist. Will was interviewed outside Café de l'Église in Paris, where he drank a café noisette.

What garment is key to your personal style?

It would have to be a tweed jacket.

How many tweed jackets do you have in your wardrobe?

Four.

How long have you had them?

I've had tweed jackets before, but the concerted push into tweediness I'd say began in 2010, only about eight years ago. I was doing a story up in the Western Isles, on the Long Island in Harris, and saw some of the new Harris tweed designs which were very controversial at that point.

What were their defining characteristics?

Shamefully, it's to do with an American entrepreneur acquiring the rights to market Harris tweed and rationalising its production. Traditionally it's produced by weavers who are on the farm, so if not personally involved with the sheep, they are close to them. They design their own tweeds; they do their own weaving; they produce their own cloth. There was a myriad of tweed terroirs and this guy started to look at what Americans were actually buying, as they're the main market for Harris tweed, and decided to rationalise the number of patterns offered into a few each season. I confess I kind of liked his patterns and I bought one when I was up there, a jacket, and that's where it began.

Are all of your tweed jackets from Harris?

Three of them are Harris and one – I suppose it's not strictly a tweed; it's more of a thick worsted wool – I had made in India, in Jaipur, when I was there for the literature festival three or four years ago. That's like a Nehru jacket with a round collar, but it's still a tweedy substance.

What is it specifically about tweed jackets that you love?

Well, I don't like the cold. I wear my tweed jacket in mid-winter with a cashmere cardigan or pullover, and then right up until May this year I was wearing a light tweed jacket and a shirt. It's totally versatile. It's a three-season coat. It takes me all the way through from September to May, so basically, it's my standard outer garment.

What does a tweed jacket convey to others?

The point about a properly cut tweed jacket is that it presents a single, defined image: I'm a middle-class brain worker who is relatively casual and doesn't have to wear a suit, that's all. It's an age thing, too. Even in my forties I would wear more sporty garments, but there comes a time where a man needs to face the realities of ageing. You have to dress much better when you're older and you have to groom much better because if you let anything slide you look dreadful.

Does it bother you if you see another man wandering around in a tweed jacket at the same function or talk as you?

It doesn't happen as much as you think. The classic look of blazer jacket or sport coat and now, increasingly, jeans and open neck shirt is ubiquitous, but the jacket material isn't always tweed by any means. People have been wearing worsted. They've been wearing wool or linen or cotton blazers. Silk jackets. Even though there are only a few main tweed styles coming out of Harris, I can only remember once or twice ever seeing another man wearing the same tweeds that I do.

Are you in the market for a new one?

I think I'll need a new one this winter.

Will you be travelling all the way up to Scotland to get one?

I'll have a look at the new Harris tweed, but I'm tempted by a Donegal or an Irish tweed just to break out a bit.

Can you describe the state of your closet?

It's spartan beyond belief. It's just the four tweed jackets. I have ten pairs of socks, ten pairs of underwear, a couple of T-shirts. I love that movie 'The Fly', the CRONENBERG version where you see that he has all the identical clothes... There was a very good feature recently, I can't remember what paper it was in, saying that it's not without accident that great minds – like me, haha – always have a remarkably simple wardrobe. It's because we realise very early on you don't want to make decisions about shit like that. I always wear the same shirts, always wear the same trousers, always wear the same jackets. The most disgusting thing I was still doing, maybe 12 or 13 years ago, and it shames me to say this, because it's really heavy: I was wearing shorts, in summer, and actually going out without a jacket. You can't do that when you are an older man. You mustn't.

When do you think the cut-off point is?

45.

No shorts after 45? Even on the beach?

Yes, you have to wear a jacket on the beach, unless you're swimming.

Have you ever been tempted to throw all your clothes away and start again?

Yes, every day! Within me is an inner dandy. And I have a cross-dressing side. I'd like to wear women's clothes. Well, not women's clothes – I'd like to wear dresses specifically. I've always fantasised about having gaudy and richly embroidered robe-like clothing. I think I'd love hats. I'd love a variety of hats. When I had hair I wished I'd grown it much longer and had it dressed much more flamboyantly. I have a completely repressed flamboyant dandy in me, although it's not repressed because I know it's there. I just sort of think, fine, I could be doing that, but then I wouldn't be writing books. It's as simple as that.

NICHOLAS DALEY and the paratrooper cargo pants

A questionnaire from June 2018 with the menswear designer. Nicholas was born in the English town of Rugby and runs his eponymous label from London.

What garment is key to your personal style?

One thing I wear a lot, and something that inspires a lot of my design work, is a pair of British paratrooper cargo pants from World War Two.

How many of these cargo pants do you have in your wardrobe?

I only have one pair of those, but my dad used to be in the Royal Marines and has passed on some of his old military cargo pants. I've also got a few similar pieces from YOHJI YAMAMOTO that I scoured the internet and saved up for when I was younger.

What are the defining specifications that make the perfect cargo pants?

I have to be comfortable in my clothes, in all senses of the word, and as a tall guy it is difficult to get that comfort with trousers. My cargos need to have a very loose, unstructured silhouette, and they need to drape or hang well.

What is it specifically about your cargo pants that you love?

I guess it is the fact that they were engineered, you know? They were made for someone to survive in, to keep my dad alive in! It's clothing at its purest and most honest. My clothes have to have a reason or come from a place of reason – it can be a detail or a particular fabric or it can have some kind of connection to me. That can be because I have made it myself, because it was given to me by my dad, or because it has a link to my Jamaican or Scottish heritage.

Does your attachment to cargos come from your father? Did you take inspiration from him and then look for that in other pieces?

Definitely, I've always had an appreciation of vintage, military and workwear because of what he had in his wardrobe. There were a couple of shops where I grew up that sold surplus military gear, so I used to buy stuff from there and over-dye it black at home, ruining all my mum's washing in the process.

Would it be fair to say that you are nostalgic in relation to fashion? That you find inspiration from the past rather than the present, or the future?

I mean, it's a bit of both really... I've always been about the harmony between past and present. I might be wearing a vintage M65 jacket but pair it with a COMME DES GARÇONS shirt and some NIKE sneaks.

Is there a garment that you used to dislike but ended up loving and wearing? When did your aversion to it turn to fondness? What changed your mind?

I would definitely say the kilt. The kilt is slowly getting there. I had one made for my Autumn & Winter 2017 collection and it was such a refreshing thing to do. Plus, it kept my mum and the Scottish side of my family happy. There is a family wedding coming up, so I'll definitely be cracking it out soon. Even now, in 2018, it is still one of the few garments in men's wardrobes that holds a reaction, which is really funny given how old it is. It still gets a response and people come up and ask questions about it.

Have you ever made a radical change in your "look"? Have you ever been tempted to get rid of all your clothes and start again from scratch?

In my earlier days I would wear a lot of streetwear brands like SUPREME, CARHARTT and STÜSSY. My dad would always go on at me to get a "proper" pair of shoes, like, a pair of CLARKS or something, and now I've moved on from being this trainer-heavy individual to collaborating with Northampton shoemakers like GEORGE COX. I think my dad is quite shocked.

What do you wear to look sexy? Do you have a pick-up look?

I've never really thought about it; you'd have to ask my girlfriend! Maybe the kilt...

JOHN BOOTH and his panther shirt

A questionnaire from December 2017 with the artist, fashion illustrator and ceramicist. John was interviewed over a sandwich in the London Review Bookshop café.

What garment is key to your personal style?

A navy cotton-and-silk MARC JACOBS shirt with golden panthers on it.

How many of these shirts do you have in your wardrobe?

Just the one.

What is it specifically about this garment that you love?

It's one of those things I have that whenever I wear it everyone goes, "Oh my God I love that." I go through phases where it maybe fits better than other times. It's like a gauge of my weight! I'm really gutted if I don't fit into it, but if I put it on and it buttons up I know I'm in better shape. I think in the winter it tends to bust open a bit more. I also just really love it; it makes me happy. It's one shirt I've really looked after. I've always had it dry-cleaned and it's aged really nicely. I think it was the first piece of expensive clothing I ever bought.

What would you say are the defining features of this shirt?

I like that it's an all-over print and on the front of the shirt where the panther goes over the button plackets it matches up perfectly with the fabric underneath to continue the panther. I think that's just the poshest thing. People actually notice that – they often come up to me and say, "Ooh the print matches up!" They get quite excited. Hang on, let me find a picture of it... There it is! [Shows picture on Google Images] Ah, it's actually MARC BY MARC, his now defunct diffusion line. I fucking love that thing. Even seeing a picture of it, some stock picture on the internet, that makes me happy. I guess it's been through quite a lot with me.

Do you know where your attachment to this garment comes from?

It was in the LIBERTY basement. The menswear bit. I was teaching a lot at Central Saint Martins at the time, around 2010 I think, and I had a bit of spare money. I felt like I deserved something. It was about £190, which I still think is a lot of money for a shirt. I went in there that day and there were a few of them on the rail because obviously people didn't like them, and that drew me in. I'm quite drawn to that sort of garment. I think it's a good sign if there's still a few left on a rail.

Why's that?

I think it's something about liking leftover things that other people don't want. Like these track pants. [Lifts leg above the table to reveal a pair of sludge-green, quilted-velvet track pants]

Oh wow! I didn't see those when I came in.

They're by DRIES VAN NOTEN. There were a lot of them left on the rail at his shop in Antwerp and I immediately wanted them. It means not many other people have them and it's also about appreciating things that maybe other people would find quite ugly. Something can look crap hanging up in a shop but then you realise you could actually pull it off. I really like DRIES. Have you seen the documentary?

I haven't.

It's good. I think he's good.

I think a lot of people think he's good.

Yeah, that's not such a radical statement! He makes some really good points in the documentary, though, like that he's never advertised. I'd never thought about that. But he doesn't need to. He has a cult following and he's always good. Even when it's crap, it's good. Like that MARILYN MONROE print. Did you see that? Fucking hell. That was the only time where I've not liked something of his. But having seen the documentary and knowing why and how he used it, now I really like it! I think he knew it was ugly and a bit tongue in cheek and just went for it. He wasn't under any illusions that it was really chic and nice... It's horrible. But he used this horrendous print of MARILYN's eyes and mouth in a way that's quite elegant.

Do you think you become more attached to clothes if you feel that you have "discovered" them yourself?

I think so. After my first big job for a fashion house I bought myself a PRADA shirt. That one with the people fighting on it by the French illustrator CHRISTOPHE CHEMIN. I just walked in and bought it, because I could. But I don't feel the same level of attachment to it as to the panther shirt. The PRADA shirt just feels a bit more crass, not least because it's so very noticeable as being PRADA from that particular season. I don't want people to go, "It's that PRADA shirt!" It feels flashy whereas the MARC BY MARC shirt was never a thing to begin with. It was just left over in the shop because nobody wanted it. I like loud stuff but not flashy stuff.

Loud but not ostentatious.

Right. There's a big difference. The latter means people know where you got it from and how much you spent on it. It signifies a lot and I find that quite off-putting. I remember when I was teaching a while ago and I came in with a pair of the new RAF SIMONS trainers on; one student immediately walked up to me and said, "How did you afford those?" I found that so weird. It was weird wearing something that people could automatically place the price of.

How do you feel when you see other men wearing a panther shirt? Are you happy to have the whole world wear "your" garment or do you prefer to stand out?

I want it to just be for me. The only other person I've ever seen wearing one was

ALASTAIR MACKIE who was wearing it in another colourway. I remember feeling annoyed at first, but then thinking, "Oh, it's a different colourway anyway, I don't care." It wasn't as attractive as my colourway.

What do you wear to look sexy? Do you have a pick-up look?

I like wearing slutty shorts! From mid April till late September I exclusively wear shorts, never trousers. I'm of quite a warm disposition – I overheat quite quickly because I'm slightly fat and northern – so I love the feeling of bare legs because it keeps me cool and I get compliments. I've been told that I've got a good, sturdy leg. Then the cellular cotton tighty-whities from SUNSPEL, which my boyfriend really likes. White MARKS & SPENCER vests are definitely part of the sexy look too. But really it's the shorts: flash a bit of hairy chest, short shorts, sorted. If it gets as far as them seeing your undies then you know it's worked.

DEAN COOK and the track pants

A questionnaire from December 2018 with the menswear buying manager of Browns. Dean was a professional footballer for many years, playing in central midfield.

What garment is key to your personal style?

Track pants.

How many pairs of track pants do you have in your wardrobe?

I've got about ten pairs of fashion ones from the likes of RICK OWENS and PRADA and untold numbers of normal sports ones from NIKE and ADIDAS.

Where does your attachment to track pants come from?

I grew up playing football. I played all the time and eventually I moved from Romford, in Essex, to Cambridge when I was about 15 years old to become an apprentice footballer for Cambridge United. I just lived in track pants and training kit. But I have one particularly formative track-pant experience that sort of shaped my life.

What was it?

I was 13, it was the school disco and I had no idea what to wear. I was completely at a loss and I had no suitable clothes. My dad played a lot of golf, so I stole his golf clothes and wore a pair of my track pants. I still remember that outfit: a white, skin-tight turtleneck, a brown SLAZENGER V-neck sweater and blue ADMIRAL track pants with the ADMIRAL logo in yellow down the sides.

Sounds good! Did anyone dance with you?

No, I don't think I was very interested in dancing at that age. But anyway, it wasn't a good look, it was an awful look! I found the whole experience of not knowing what to wear and not having any clothes so stressful and embarrassing that I decided I was going to make an effort to understand clothes and style. And I think, in a way, that moment led to me working in fashion.

How exactly did you go about transforming your style?

I went straight to the newsagents and I found two magazines. One was 'The Face' and the other was a magazine called 'Unique'. Tell me if you ever find a copy because I've been looking for copies online but it's impossible; if you google "unique magazine" it just comes up with loads of random stuff. 'Unique' was very important for me. It was different to 'The Face', it was British but more focused on Italian fashion: ARMANI, VERSACE, BEST COMPANY CLOTHING, etcetera.

Were you a bit of an Italophile?

I was, yeah. I used to advise everyone in my football team on which Italian brands they should be buying and all my salary went on clothes. I remember going to Browns on South Molton Street in the mid '80s and buying my first pair of ARMANI JEANS. They cost £50 and I was only earning £25 a week playing for Cambridge.

Have you ever made a radical change in your look? Would you be tempted to start again from scratch?

After I stopped playing football in the '90s and started working in fashion, I worked in wholesale for brands. So I've always taken the lead from where I work. I was at DONNA KARAN and I wore a lot of black cashmere. Then I went to PRADA and had a very minimal PRADA look going on, same with when I was at JIL SANDER.

What PRADA era were you there for?

Around the time that NEIL BARRETT launched men's and they were just developing PRADA SPORT. They didn't have the red stripe yet but they were making this quite groundbreaking sport-fashion thing. I wore a lot of V-neck sweaters, light blue shirts, technical fabric trousers and oversized shoes. It was a really exciting time to be there. Here's a question, when you go home, do you change and put a pair of track pants on?

Erm, no. I don't. I'm quite happy in trousers.

See, I always change into track pants in the home. Partly for comfort and partly through habit. Even if I've worn track pants to the office during the day, I get changed into a different pair when I get home. Usually I go for an old worn-in pair of NIKE or ADIDAS ones because they're most comfortable.

What does your wardrobe look like?

It is very organised, but by category, not by colour. All jackets together, all sweaters together, shirts together, T-shirts together, long-sleeved shirts together. I have a double wardrobe with all my clothes in and then another for all my coats, and then a drawer for underwear and socks. I also have an entire chest of drawers just for sport socks. I'm obsessed. A conservative estimate would be I've got about 75 pairs.

Do you have an amazing wardrobe management tip?

Never hang a sweater.

Not even on a special, grippy hanger?

No, never ever.

Where do you keep them? Don't they take up loads of room?

Folded. I fold the finer gauge ones in a drawer, and then the chunkier ones are folded under the hanging space in my wardrobe.

Do you have a special folding technique?

Of course. I go shoulder over, arm down the middle, other shoulder over, other arm down the middle. Then fold in half. But with the heavier gauge ones I don't do that because they would pile up really high. So I fold them in half, then leave the arms by the side and just lay them flat. You know, when you leave home at 15 and have to live with another family, you grow up quite quickly. You get very good at being neat and folding things.

HED MAYNER and the XL white button-down shirt

A questionnaire from January 2017 with an Israeli menswear designer. Hed runs his eponymous brand from Israel's second most populous city, Tel Aviv.

What garment is key to your personal style?

XL white button-down shirts.

How many of these shirts do you have in your wardrobe?

Seven.

What is it specifically about this garment that you love?

I love how sometimes in the sun the whiteness of the shirt looks so light and bright. I also love the way that cotton feels on the skin.

What are the defining specifications for the perfect button-down shirt?

Smooth surface, slightly transparent, and large. I like it when the fabric looks like it barely touches the body.

Do you know where your attachment to them comes from?

As a child, I remember my father only wearing a uniform of work clothes because he was a metalworker. I think that maybe the white button-down shirt is my practical working uniform since I spend so much of my time in the studio.

How do you feel when you see other men wearing the same thing? Are you happy to have the whole world wear "your" garment or do you prefer to stand out?

I once saw more than 500 people dressed in the same white button-down shirt and standing together in the same space. It looked scary and liberating at the same time. I think this garment always looks so different for each person.

Who or what do you look at for style inspiration? Do you look at fashion?

I look at the different cultures around me and the possibility of these cultures to mix or not; I look at the way people are moving around the globe and what they are bringing or taking with them.

Can you describe the state of your closet? Is it tidy, messy, super organised and are your clothes folded, boxed, grouped by colour or season, etcetera?

Quite organised and limited – you could fit all the items in one suitcase. I actually don't wear most of my clothes; they are stored in boxes in my studio or at the warehouse.

Have you ever made a radical change in your "look"? Have you ever been tempted to get rid of all your clothes and start again from scratch?

When I was 14, I went through a period where I only bought clothes in stores for large men, where they sell sizes like 4XL, 5XL, etcetera. It was a very strange look because I was very small and everything was huge on me – and belted. I made my entire wardrobe this way, but it stopped after some time.

Have you ever considered settling on a strict uniform and if so, what would it be?

When I spend many hours working, I usually wear the same thing for weeks, only because it helps me to concentrate.

Does your work influence what you wear?

Usually during the development of a collection the work influences the way I dress because I am often trying things on; during the fitting I am wearing the pattern or the early prototype around the studio.

What do you wear to look sexy?

I think sex is something that is always there, somehow.

What amazing tip for wardrobe management can you share?

Give other people the things that you don't wear anymore.

FRÀNÇOIS MARRY and the airplane blanket

A questionnaire from May 2017 with the Brussels-based singer. Frànçois is in a band called Frànçois and the Atlas Mountains.

What garment is key to your personal style?

Airplane blankets that I wear as scarves.

How many different airplane blankets do you have in your wardrobe?

I have a collection of six different airplane blankets. My favourite is from ETHIOPIAN AIRLINES.

What is it specifically about airplane blankets that you love?

They're light, warm, you can take a nap with them, hide from the wind or even use them as a picnic blanket.

What are the defining specifications for the perfect airplane blanket?

They have to come from an exotic country and the logo has to look like it has remained unchanged since the 1970s.

Have you ever seen anyone else wearing an airplane blanket?

I've never seen any other man wearing

airplane blanket scarves. But last year I found out my aunt has an airplane blanket collection! We swapped a few items, as we both had spares. I exchanged an AMERICAN AIRLINES one for an AIR FRANCE one.

Do you have a dress code for work? Does your work influence what you wear?

Work for me is being a musician. Clothes I wear on stage have to be light enough to dance and sweat in and loose enough to sing in, with lots of air swelling my belly. We've started a collaboration with the designer JULIEN DAVID. He lent us clothes and we wear them on stage and during promo. So I guess that's my new work outfit. Although when I write and compose at home, in my cold Brussels flat, I often wear a woolen djellaba a Sufi singer gave me in Morocco.

Who or what do you look at for style inspiration? Do you look at fashion?

I only started looking at fashion when I met HEDI SLIMANE a couple of years ago. I was intrigued.

Have you ever considered settling on a strict uniform and if so, what would it be?

I went through a phase of wearing only white shirts. That was when I lost my job as an assistant and decided to be a full-time poor musician. It was a way to reassure myself. I thought it made me look less unemployed.

ANGELO FLACCAVENTO and the blue blazer

A questionnaire from September 2016 with the famed fashion critic. Angelo is from Ragusa and splits his time between that Sicilian city and Milan.

What garment is key to your personal style?

The blue blazer, either single or double-breasted.

How many blue blazers do you have in your wardrobe?

I'd say around 20 in total, both winter and summer versions.

What is it about blazers, blue ones specifically, that you love?

I think a tailored blazer gives presence and posture, but is also quite easy to wear. A blazer gives an immediate impression of appropriateness. Blue is the quintessential masculine colour: deep but not stark, academic yet easy going.

Do you know where your attachment to them comes from? Is it something from your youth, or something you picked up from a specific person? When, who?

I was given a blue blazer for my First Holy Communion and I loved it. Another one followed shortly after. I think I was drawn early on by the presence of the blue blazer; it is gently commanding.

How do you feel when you see other men wearing the same thing? Are you happy to have the whole world wear blue blazers or do you prefer to stand out?

The garment does not feel exclusively personal to me. I would surely recommend it if asked for advice.

Do you look at fashion for style inspiration?

I don't look at fashion. Instead I like to look at portraits of artists – they ooze the charm of a man who makes things and gets his hands dirty. I love the style of DAVID HOCKNEY in the '60s, and I find FRANCESCO CLEMENTE wonderful. Curiously enough, neither of them are known for wearing blue blazers.

Can you describe the state of your closet? Is it tidy, messy, super organised?

My wardrobe is very tidy. I keep it grouped by colour and divided into two seasons: Spring/Summer and Autumn/Winter.

Have you ever considered settling on a strict uniform and if so, what would it be? Would you consider it a relief?

I would love to have a uniform, preferably something blue and Maoist. I think it would come as a great relief.

Is there a garment that you used to dislike but ended up loving and wearing?

In my street-kid phase I was wearing lots of T-shirts and I thought the idea of a blazer in the summer was absolute torture. Now I've discovered that, if you choose the right super-light wool, a blazer can feel great even under the glaring sun.

Do you have a pick-up look?

I don't, but I've noticed that the more academic I look, the better the effect.

Do you choose what you'll wear in advance? Like, the night before?

I try to, but invariably I change my mind in the morning.

Who do you talk to when you want to talk about clothes?

My partner; he is a good listener and I like his point of view.

What amazing tip for wardrobe management or maintenance can you share?

I air my clothes a lot and brush them from time to time. That's it.

ALEX TIEGHI-WALKER and the patterned shirt

A questionnaire from September 2016 with the 29-year-old creative director. Alex works in San Francisco and edits the 'Anonymous Sex Journal'.

What garment is key to your personal style?

Principally, I wear heavily patterned shirts, and have done most of my life: LIBERTY prints, Hawaiian shirts, Asian silk shirts. There are photos of me as a kid wearing tie-dye T-shirts and African prints. The look must have stuck!

How many of these printed shirts do you have in your wardrobe?

I own about eight Hawaiian shirts, and a dozen or so floral LIBERTY prints, four patterned djellabas, a shirt decorated with Babar motifs, one with bottles of rum and safari maps, one with GAUGUINesque women making baskets, and another one with people skiing down a slope.

What is it specifically about patterned shirts that you love?

I'm a totally uncoordinated person, so am always spilling juice, wine or food down myself. My pens always leak in my pockets, I sit down on muddy grass, eat with my fingers and wipe my hands on whatever clothes I'm wearing. The patterns on the shirts tend to hide a lot of those mishaps, a bit like the heavily patterned materials used on public transport seats. In general, I magpie towards detailed patterns – for the home too. I find them very beautiful and stimulating.

How do you feel when you see other men wearing the same type of shirts? Are you happy to have the whole world wear "your" shirts or do you prefer to stand out?

There was a phase when Hawaiian shirts became trendy, and I do see other people wearing LIBERTY prints, but they are usually women. I suppose floral prints tend to be seen as less masculine. I like that I'm one of the few men I know who wears patterns. A lot of people compliment me on the more interesting or intricate fabrics.

Do you know where your attachment to these shirts comes from? Is it something from your youth, or something you picked up from a specific person? When, who?

My mother travelled a lot so our house was filled with bright, colourful patterns and prints. I've also travelled to, and lived in, a lot of places where complex textile design is part of the visual discourse: India, Tibet, Bolivia, Morocco, the Wild West. My aunt had WILLIAM MORRIS wallpaper and fabrics in her London home, and my grandmother collected ROYAL CROWN DERBY china, so I've always been surrounded by patterns and print, and by people not afraid to indulge in them.

How are your shirts organised inside your wardrobe? Are you tidy or messy?

I'm not one for folding or hanging items on hangers – or ironing clothes – so all my shirts hang on S hooks on the wall like coats in a cloakroom. I used to have a one-in, one-out clothing policy to keep my wardrobe and storage clear of crap, but that hasn't been happening lately.

What amazing tip for wardrobe management or maintenance can you share?

I'd say the one-in, one-out policy, because it helps you realise which clothes you truly value and stops you buying clothes which aren't really that special.

Have you ever made a radical change in your "look"? Have you ever been tempted to get rid of all your clothes and start again from scratch?

I think the main change has been ageing. In my early twenties I used to wear tighter clothing, but now I prefer loose-fitting items and I wear a woolly hat more often (to hide my growing bald patch). Since moving to California I've also lightened my wardrobe. Before I used to wear patterned shirts as my first layer, topped off with a plain shirt. Now I wear a plain T-shirt topped off with a patterned shirt.

Have you ever considered settling on a strict uniform? Would you consider it a relief, or would it be a loss of options?

I guess I already wear a strict uniform because the composition of my outfit rarely changes, even if the individual items do. I think I'm too restless and need too much stimulation to ever reduce my wardrobe to a simple uniform; even at home I'm constantly repainting, moving furniture around, experimenting, changing things. It frustrates my roommates but the change excites me.

What do you wear to look sexy? Do you have a pick-up look?

Funnily enough, when I want to look attractive I generally eschew my day-to-day look and wear all black or navy. It makes me look a bit thinner, I think. I'm not sure I'm very sexy even at the best of times; I definitely look more friendly and approachable than seductive and alluring.

What ultimately signifies your style of dressing?

Shirts aside, everything else I wear is very practical and plain, like large navy smocks, beaten corduroys, oversized cotton jackets, heavy workwear, boots, denim and thick woollen socks. Because I work on a farm a couple of days a week, and also spend a lot of time making things, or being outdoors, I like clothes that look okay dirty. A friend once said that I dress like a third class passenger on the Titanic.

TEERABUL SONGVICH and his outrageous hats

A questionnaire from April 2018 with a Thai pattern cutter. Teerabul's most famous creation, the mirror dress, has been worn by Kate Moss, Björk and the late Isabella Blow.

What garment is key to your personal style?

It's hard, because I like clothes in general. But I think the thing that I would associate with myself the most would be headwear. Hats and caps and things like that. Even if I go out to get milk in the morning I need to wear a hat – it's such a habit now. If I don't have a hat on I feel exposed.

How many hats are in your wardrobe?

Over 100. I collect all sorts of hats. I like Turkish caps. I've got lots of sailor hats, Spanish hats. I've got a shelf full of hats above my bed, I've got boxes and boxes in my wardrobe and loads in the garage. They're everywhere.

What is it about hats that you love?

I like dressing up. I never really plan my outfits; I just throw lots of fun things on and hats are the cherry on top of the cake. Hats also set the overall mood of what I'm wearing. If I want to look jolly and happy I'll wear quite a big hat. If I feel I want to have more of a relaxed, quiet day, I'll wear a smaller one.

What are the defining specifications that make the perfect hat?

It changes, depending on the season. In summer I wear a lot of straw hats because they're breathable and airy. When it gets to winter I wear more felt hats. At the moment I'm going into my garage and digging out my warmest headwear.

Do you know where your attachment to hats comes from? Is it something from your youth, or something you picked up from a specific person? When, who?

I was born in Bangkok and I moved to London about 23 years ago to study fashion. I don't have any hair and I come from a warm country, so at first, hats were a necessity because I found the weather so cold and needed to cover my head. I initially started wearing baseball hats; then I started buying some straw hats. Those were my first steps and it escalated from there. Then I started working and getting more money and I started buying more expensive and bizarre hats. My hats have been getting bigger and more outrageous ever since.

So your hat collection started as something practical and has gradually snowballed into an obsession?

Yes. It's a bit like... Well, I don't take drugs, but I imagine it's a bit like taking drugs! At the beginning just a little will do and by the end you need something bigger. People don't wear hats so much anymore, so when you wear a big hat, like a big WESTWOOD hat, people always comment and take pictures and have a look. I don't mind. Macho men like to look at me in disapproving ways and all the women tend to compliment me.

Don't you sometimes get compliments from macho men?

Yes, sometimes. Mostly when they're drunk! They'll come up to me and say, "I really like what you're wearing." I can never tell if they're being honest or cynical. But I like dressing up and I know that's part of it. I don't dress up to please everyone.

How do you feel when you see other men wearing the same thing? Are you happy to have the whole world wear "your" sort of hats or do you prefer to stand out?

I really like it. When someone wears an outrageous hat and sees someone else wearing one too, they sort of nod to each other in recognition. We know what it's like wearing hats like that in a country where people don't even wear simple hats anymore. I always ask if I can take a picture.

Oh wow, so there's a secret outrageous hat society?

Yes!

NOVELIST and the tracksuit

A questionnaire from April 2018 with the 21-year-old south London grime MC and producer. Novelist has his very own label called MMMYEH Records, and his real name is Kojo Kankam.

What garment is key to your personal style?

I'm going to say the tracksuit.

How many tracksuits do you have in your wardrobe?

Ah, I couldn't tell you. Definitely over ten.

What is it specifically about this garment that you love?

I just feel that no matter where you are in life you can't go wrong with a tracksuit. They're simple and plain, not too expensive. But if I told you honestly, it's about comfort, and also about being able to look nice and healthy. Looking healthy at the same time as being comfortable is cool, man, I like it.

I've never thought about specifically trying to look healthy when you get dressed, but

I guess it makes a lot of sense.

Well, I've got an athletic physique. If I was a bit chubbier or, I don't know, of a different stature, then I might not want to wear tracksuits so much. They just suit me. I'd say comfort first, and they just happen to look good on me as well, you know what I mean?

What are the defining specifications that make the perfect tracksuit?

They are predominantly from NIKE; there are some other bits and bobs, but let's say generally NIKE. Usually in darker colours, matching tops and bottoms, always. If I'm honest with you bro, I wish companies made more colourful stuff. In England there's generally a very dark tone to the clothes that come out of sports shops. I'm actually a colourful person. Another thing I'll say is that I'm not a fan of clothing that is too tight. I like to feel free in my clothes, so I get tracksuits that are a bit on the looser side. I like clothes that give me a bit of space.

Are they mostly cotton? Or nylon?

Cotton mostly. The nylon ones I would call a shell suit. I love shell suits, too. I think of tracksuits as cotton bottoms and a cotton hoodie pullover, whereas a shell suit is nylon and the top has a zip. I wear shell suits when the weather's a bit warmer.

I sometimes see guys in two pairs of tracksuit bottoms. Like, a really massive pair on top that are lower down around the bum and another smaller pair underneath, is that something you do?

Yeah, straight! That's not even for style, that's for warmth. I'm Afro-Caribbean, born here but my mum's from Antigua and my dad's from Ghana so, like, I'm born in England but I feel my body type is for hot weather. I need to stay warm.

Do you know where your attachment to this garment comes from? Is it something from your youth, or something you picked up from a specific person? When, who?

It's since I was a youth. I can't say this time or that time, but since I was a little kid, a tracksuit is just what I got put in. I'd always have to wear little polo tops too, but I feel that's what every little kid has to wear. I left the polo tops behind and kept the tracksuits.

Can you describe the state of your closet? Is it tidy, messy, super organised and are your clothes grouped by colour or season?

My wardrobe is quite neat. I like order in my life. I've got three wardrobes that are pieced together... How can I describe it? It's like a corner piece: you've got one in the centre, one on the left, one on the right... This is a weirdly hard question.

Apologies!

Nah, it's actually interesting to think about. Because, being a musician, people are constantly offering to send me clothing. I've gotten to the stage now where I'd rather take less and just wear something plain. I'm happy just wearing a white T-shirt. I didn't grow up with a lot of money, so when I came into money I wanted to get all the things I'd ever wanted. But I've gotten to the stage now where I've got enough. I've come to the realisation that there are much more important things in life than clothes. You're better off giving them to charity. I've got a lot of clothes bagged up right now, actually.

Have you ever made a radical change to your look?

Not really, I've always been quite consistent. I'd say I've started wearing more workwear. CARHARTT, DICKIES, stuff like that. I've always been into those styles, but I didn't know where to get anything like that as a kid. All I knew was JD SPORTS, PRIMARK, SPORTS DIRECT. It was all a bit of a mystery. I'm into a simple look. It's powerful.

Do you have a dress code for work?

I still wear tracksuits, and then a bum bag over my shoulder. I always put my phone in my bum bag; you don't want your phone falling out on stage. My bum bags are mainly from NIKE, but I also have a good EASTPAK one. Back in the days we would all wear gun-pouch bum bags.

What's a gun-pouch bum bag?

I think they were called gun pouches... We got them from the market. They go over your shoulder and tuck under your armpit. You'd keep your cigarettes in there and whatever else you had on you.

Oh, like a holster?

Yeah a holster! They looked good, actually. They've a got a bit of a detective look.

HERMÈS do good leather holster wallets if you're looking for a fancy one.

I'm googling it now. I'm definitely going to bring that look back this summer. Keep an eye out at festivals.

LEWIS DALTON GILBERT and the eBay wardrobe

A questionnaire from April 2018 with a creative producer for Frieze, the art publication and art fair phenomenon. Lewis is from London and is still averse to the colour beige.

What garment is key to your personal style?

My interests vary month to month. For example, I'm really into blazers with quite a high neck and four buttons at the moment, and last month I was all about wide-legged trousers. But I'd say the defining factor of my wardrobe is that 90 per cent of it is made up of eBay purchases. It's the first place I'll look for something.

Do you know where your attachment to eBay comes from?

I think it started when I was a student and I was being a bit thrifty and a bit frugal. But now it just seems like common sense, slash, an addiction. I know exactly what I want and I don't really like wandering around shops. I'm not an aimless shopper. I don't like going into stores, trying something on. Maybe you aren't wearing the right kind of clothes to get a sense of what a garment really looks like and you risk it and take it home, but it turns out it doesn't really go with anything. I just find that environment quite stressful. But with eBay you're in the comfort of your own home, you're researching and looking into things. You can spend a lot of time on it. I find it quite easy and therapeutic.

But isn't eBay even worse in terms of risk because you can't try on or touch the clothes before you buy them and often they're so badly shot?

Well I actually find that quite exciting. Also, I have faith in the designers that I'm looking for. It doesn't always pay off, but I know my size and I'll see something and just risk it. Recently I bought an ISSEY MIYAKE blazer. I got it for £37. When it came it was so much nicer than it was in the images. I find that happens a lot. You need to be willing to take a bit of a gamble and you need to have checkboxes in your head, where it's, like: this designer, in this colour, and it's my size. How wrong can it be? The biggest gambles that I've made have usually paid off. And if it turns up and it's really horrible, you just take a better picture and re-sell it!

What kind of garments do you typically buy from eBay?

The specifics vary, but generally I wear black. What's nice about that is it makes it easier to shop. It means that you focus on different things, maybe looking at certain fabrics or the shape of an item of clothing instead of getting distracted by its pattern or colour. I wear some colours but they're usually muted, like a dull khaki or, at a push, maybe a navy. But it's such a dark navy that it's almost black. This year I bought a beige COMME DES GARÇONS jacket, but even beige is too out there for me and I've only worn it once. I'll probably sell it in order to buy another pair of black trousers.

It's great that you consider beige too jazzy.

Honestly, it feels like such a huge detachment. Whenever I wear beige I feel like COCO THE CLOWN.

What is it about eBay that's so addictive?

I think the trick of eBay is that it makes it feel like it's a really personal experience. You'll see an item of clothing and it's your size and you're almost convinced it's for you. Even the language they use to message you, "You've won!" – but, like, I haven't won it, I've paid for it. I've literally been sat here refreshing the browser to make sure I have the privilege of buying it. The way you search for things also makes it very involving and makes it feel like an accomplishment when you find a hidden gem or an amazing seller. I have an incredible seller from Japan who I follow and I'm not telling anyone their name! It's top secret.

I was bidding on something the other weekend. I'm so embarrassed to admit this but I was in the cinema when the listing was due to finish and I ran out of the film to put my final bid in. I won, but it was a bizarre mixture of feeling a bit elated and a bit ashamed.

I totally get that. Still, it's better than the other side of eBay where you lose something because you've been on the phone to your mum. It's deep, and the resentment goes on for a long while. If I've missed something because of someone else, it's not an easy thing to get over. Listings are normally a week. So, you see it early in the week, you start watching it, you've been mentally putting it into your wardrobe, thinking about what you'd wear it with, where it's going to go. And then when you lose it...it's brutal.

It just evaporates from your life.

Yes. From your virtual fantasy wardrobe.

What's the last thing you bought on eBay?

Let's have a look... It was a green ACNE bomber jacket, from Lithuania.

Has it arrived yet?

No, it's supposed to arrive next Friday, according to the tracking.

Have you ever considered settling on a strict uniform and if so, what would it be?

I think my wardrobe must already look quite regimented and uniform to other people. But I think even in a wardrobe of very similar things there are still variations, even if other people don't immediately notice them. Even if it doesn't necessarily look that different to the naked eye, I think these variations can really change your mood. A lot of the time people will say to me, "You don't need another pair of black trousers!" and I'm, like, "Why not? Why shouldn't I have loads of black trousers?" I love wearing black trousers in many different styles because there are many different occasions that you'll go to, there are many different feelings that you'll feel and there are a hundred different moods that you'll be in. It's great to have a pair of black trousers for every one.

PAUL GORMAN and the baker pants

A questionnaire from August 2017 with the writer and cultural chronicler. Paul wrote about the history of 'The Face' and is working on a biography of Malcolm McLaren.

What garment is key to your personal style?

I want to talk about baker pants. Do you know what they are?

The big checkered trousers that chefs wear?

Oh no, not those. Baker pants are American military trousers. They're called baker pants because I imagine at some point bakers wore them. But I'm not sure.

How many pairs of baker pants do you have in your wardrobe?

I've got three pairs.

What is it specifically about this garment that you love?

They're incredibly comfortable – cool in the summer, warm in the winter. I like the straight leg and the high rise of them as well. It's a masculine trouser but it also looks great on women. I've worn them since I was 16.

What are the defining specifications that make the perfect example of this garment?

They should be flat-fronted and straight-legged. I like them in olive and made from cotton sateen, which is quite shiny when it starts off but gets very soft over time. They've got square-oblong pockets that are visible and a button fly. I have one pair from the Vietnam War and they have a mysterious tear in them which I always wonder about.

Do you know where your attachment to this garment comes from?

Yes, it was the summer of 1976. I'd been to see ROXY MUSIC the previous autumn at the Empire Pool in Wembley. It was when 'Love is the Drug' was a big hit and for their tour ANTONY PRICE had designed outfits around this G.I. theme. BRYAN FERRY had these smart, straight-legged khaki trousers, a buttoned khaki shirt with epaulettes and a tie tucked into the third button on the front of his shirt. I saw those straight-legged army trousers and went to an army surplus shop in Hendon to try and find some. I picked up a full khaki shirt and trouser set just like BRYAN, but I also found a pair of olive-coloured baker pants and I completely fell in love with them. There's that unbeatable feeling when you've found something really nice, really hard-wearing, almost by chance.

How do you feel when you see other men wearing the same thing?

As original baker pants are increasingly hard to come by, I actually don't tell anyone where I buy mine now. One thing that I found out retrospectively was that MALCOLM McLAREN loved these trousers, too. I knew him later in life and he told me this story of when he went to Florida in 1974 with the NEW YORK DOLLS. They split up and he and SYLVAIN SYLVAIN drove to New Orleans and they needed appropriate clothing just to get around so they went to an army surplus store and they bought baker pants because they were really comfortable and you can just wear them with anything. He brought a pair back to London and they became the basis for bondage trousers.

No way!

Yeah! They've got exactly the same design but they put double zips in the back which tightened them.

Who or what do you look at for style inspiration? Do you look at fashion?

PETER YORK is my style hero. He's actually my hero all round. Without him and NICK KENT, I would never have become a writer. He's just so well dressed and so amazingly presented. And really smart and funny and still kind of avante. You can't contain him within any kind of respectability.

It sounds like you have been quite consistent in how you dress, seeing as you've worn the same type of trousers since you were 16, but have you ever made a radical change to your "look"?

In the early '90s I was living in Los Angeles and got into this scene that was all about a rat-pack, Vegas lounge lizard look: sharkskin suits, money clips and buckled red fake snakeskin shoes. You can see it in the mid '90s movie 'Swingers' with a young VINCE VAUGHN, but that was a bit late and more of a Hollywood fantasy. It was a reaction against acid house and casual wear, and at the same time it was a bit gritty, a bit dirty realism. I was hanging out with people like EL VEZ, the Mexican Elvis, who I later managed for a while, actually. That sort of people. Very gritty but quite dressed up.

DEVENDRA BANHART and his three scarves

A questionnaire from January 2017 with the 35-year-old singer-songwriter. Devendra was born in Texas and spent his early childhood in Venezuela, before moving to California.

What garment is key to your personal style?

At the moment, there are three scarves. One is a cotton scarf made by one of the Japanese brand SEILIN & CO.'s many branches, called Mother Nature. I'm wearing it now and I'm feeling satisfactorily neck-protected. The second is actually a dish rag my mother gave to me; it's paper thin with a few holes. I remember her drying dishes with it. The last one is a vintage YVES SAINT LAURENT cotton scarf. It has a gentle Mediterranean motif on it: a cubist rendition of VENUS DE MILO with a block of blue sea behind it.

Only three?

The reason I only have three scarves is because it is so delightful to give them away on a whim. Unfortunately, I gave away all of the beautiful scarves my mother gave me. I always had a scarf or two in my purse to give away, and then I had none left. But I've held on to these three for a good few months now. I really do love scarves.

What are the defining specifications that make the perfect scarf?

The touch, smell or sight of it must give you an immediate sense of familiarity – something eerie and maternal.

Do you know where your attachment to scarves comes from? Is it something from your youth, or something you picked up from a specific person?

It's a lifelong attempt at embodying, or even approximating, a particular archetype that I like to call "Vitamin Dad meets Auntie Art Teacher."

Can you describe the state of your closet?

I keep distilling it. Donating is fun and feels good. Once every few months I tend to fill up a bag and drop it off at the local Out of the Closet. They're a great charity that supports the Aids Healthcare Foundation and provides free HIV testing.

Have you ever considered settling on a strict uniform and if so, what would it be?

Inconsistency was de rigueur during most of my adolescence (which according to every girlfriend I've ever had is an ongoing phase for me). At the moment, I love the ease of a monochromatic outfit, any colour. Jumpsuits are always good. I recently saw DAVID STEINDL-RAST, the amazing Benedictine monk, speak and that brown on cream get-up is so fresh!

Do you have a dress code for work?

I used to dress up for the grocery store, dress higher up for a party, and dress way down for a show. But now I have no idea and anything goes each day. However, "Japanese Gardener" is always the go-to look..

Do you choose your outfits in advance? Like, the night before?

No, I'm a three-seconds-before sorta gal.

HARRY MUNDY and his 6-foot-long belt

A questionnaire from June 2018 with Vivienne Westwood's senior menswear designer. Harry was interviewed while enjoying a pint of beer in a West London pub.

What garment is key to your personal style?

Oddly enough, a belt. I wear one every single day.

A lot of people never think about their belt. It's so rarely seen, unless you tuck your shirt into your trousers.

I hate seeing belt loops without a belt in them. It looks...weird.

Exactly how many belts do you have in your wardrobe?

Two. One brown and one black.

That's all you need really. What is it specifically about these belts that you love?

They are so simple, but so much craft goes into their making – I get them made for my own brand by a master saddle-and-bridle maker. Knowing that a lovely man in Worcestershire has applied a lifetime of knowledge to make something that seems so simple is a wonderful thing.

What are the defining specifications that make these the perfect belts?

They are just over 6 feet long, so they go around your body twice, which is rather unusual. It took me a long time to figure out a way to wrap 6 feet of leather around myself and look cool. Even now when I sell them, I have to send out instructions to customers. They are made from traditional bridle leather, a material that is built to withstand every element when you are out clattering around on a horse. In theory they should last 100 years at the very least.

Do you know where your attachment to

these belts comes from? Is it something from your youth, or something you picked up from a specific person? When, who?

My mother used to be a punk singer in Paris and wore something very similar – I completely fell in love with it aged 15.

How do you feel when you see other men wearing the same thing? Are you happy to have the whole world wear "your" garment or do you prefer to stand out?

I'm not someone who is precious about my ideas – I borrow so much from so many different sources and areas of inspiration that it would be hypocritical to be precious. If I saw someone with something similar I would probably think, "Damn, you're stylish," and go and have a chat. We would probably get on quite well!

Have you ever made a radical change in your "look"?

So many times. I used to be a little punk with knee-high boots and piercings all over my face, but then I spent a fair bit of time working on Savile Row and wore a bespoke suit and a much more sensible haircut! Now I'm kind of an amalgamation of the two.

Did you get rid of all your clothes and start again from scratch each time you changed your look?

No, I could never get rid of everything. I'm someone who forms huge attachments to things. The waistcoat I'm wearing now belonged to my great aunt and I wear it pretty much every day. Also, a lot of the pieces I've designed over the years have a particular kind of emotional attachment, no matter how terrible they are. I find it enjoyable to see how I have evolved.

Is there a garment that you used to dislike but ended up loving and wearing? When did your aversion to it turn to fondness? What changed your mind?

Weirdly, I never wore a lot of T-shirts until recently. I think it was a bit of a hangover from the formality of Savile Row, but I have to say that a big baggy T-shirt is fucking brilliant. I feel so much more comfortable, physically and mentally.

JOSHUA SEIDNER and the white T-shirt

A questionnaire from March 2017 with the 36-year-old conceptual artist. Joshua is based in New York City's Chinatown.

What garment is key to your personal style?

A white T-shirt.

How many white T-shirts do you have in your wardrobe?

Four or five clean ones, swapped out pretty consistently, and two or three holey, shredded ones that stick around.

What is it specifically about white T-shirts that you love?

They're sincere. It's an understatement. It's a warm blankness that we know and wear so we make it a screen to project an idea or identity upon. A white T-shirt looks good when clean, crisp and dry, but may be even better ripped, stained or wet. It reminds everyone of something and me of MARLON BRANDO in 'A Streetcar Named Desire'.

Who or what do you typically look at for style inspiration?

Belgian tourists in summer, overgrown boy scouts, dirt-kneed preppies, gay greasers, casual skinheads and Mexican MORRISSEY fans. I also have a thing for Greek sailors, Dickensian dudes in Chinatown, militant Ashkenazis and soft Sephardis.

Can you describe the state of your closet?

It's organised, but only because I've got a lot of Virgo rising.

Have you ever considered settling on a strict uniform and if so, what would it be?

I'm not an architect.

What do you wear to look sexy?

The idea that clothes are something sexy is such a dull pressure. "Sexy" is just marketing and magazine-speak. Clothes don't spell sex, despite all those on-the-nose elements like leather and straps and tear-away buttons down the sides of track pants that try to imply otherwise. I guess the only thing to wear when you want to look sexy is less.

What underwear do you wear?

Clean underwear, always.

What defines your style of dressing?

I think that we're finally at the point where that set and staid notion of masculinity has gone out of fashion. Men aren't wearing gender in the same self-serious way as before. And accordingly, my style suggests a sort of manifest identity. It's post-personality; it's failed actor, and it half-heartedly plays with performance and the remnants of male roles invented last century.

LUCIEN PAGÈS and the espadrille

A questionnaire from August 2017 with the PR mastermind. Lucien founded his eponymous fashion public relations and communications agency in 2006 and is based in Paris.

What garment is key to your personal style?

The espadrille.

How many espadrilles do you have in your wardrobe?

I don't have loads, maybe five pairs. I have some in Paris and some at my home in the south of France.

What is it specifically about espadrilles that you love?

I really like to travel with them as they are very easy to fit in your suitcase.

Do you know where your attachment to espadrilles comes from? Is it something from your youth, or something you picked up from a specific person? When, who?

I come from Vialas, which is the little village in the south of France where espadrilles originally come from. When I was a child all the men wore espadrilles. There is always someone selling espadrilles among the fruit and vegetables at the market in Vialas. I remember my grandfather used to wear them – he was a pastry chef and his speciality was mille-feuille. For a while I really didn't like espadrilles because they were the shoes of my grandfather and I didn't want to dress like him. I was young and he was old-fashioned and quite tough. But then, later on, I developed a liking for them. That can happen sometimes – you eventually learn to love these objects you once rejected, or that embarrassed you. In fact, I think sometimes the more you hate something, the more you end up loving it later.

What are the defining specifications of the the perfect espadrilles?

They should have a rope sole and the upper part is usually canvas, which makes them breathable. When I wear them I like to squash the heel down, like those GUCCI shoes. That's always been the cool way of wearing them. Unfortunately, the cheaper ones in the south of France have started being made with plastic soles, which just isn't right, but thankfully, since JONATHAN ANDERSON has been at LOEWE, they have made good ones each season. I have a pair of LOEWE ones in brown suede.

Are you happy to have the whole world wear espadrilles or do you prefer to stand out?

I am happy but I don't like seeing people wearing them in Paris. I would never wear them in Paris. For me, the espadrille is linked to being in nature: the seaside, mountains, rivers. They have thin soles and give you the sensation of being very close to the ground. It's quite a nice sensation in nature but in the city I think it's dirty.

Who or what do you typically look at for style inspiration?

I look at men in the street, mostly. I'm not one of those people (continued on p. 44)

Live from CHARLES JEFFREY's wardrobe

What started as a fun club night called Loverboy soon became the sensational label for Charles Jeffrey's unlimited fashion fantasies. The young Scottish designer is now one of London Fashion Week's biggest draws. His dazzling success contrasts nicely with the simple walled unit at his home in London where he stores his assortment of vintage treasures and fabulous one-offs. It's a good starting point for an intimate chat about clothes, and what's underneath them. Interview by ELIOT HAWORTH.

I understand you've had a big wardrobe clear-out recently?

Yes, I had way too many clothes in there and the hanging pole just collapsed, so I decided to do a bit of an edit. I got rid of a lot and also thought about what I wear most often. A lot of things are now folded and stored out of the way, and I've kept just the things I'm wearing most at the moment.

Do you accumulate a lot?

I'm definitely a hoarder. I go through stages where I hoard, and then I have moments where I suddenly decide I need to get rid of a lot. But I do find it hard to get rid of things. My process of design involves working with old clothes and old toiles and cutting them up. It's my primary research.

That must make it hard to know what to throw away.

You're right. My studio manager NAOMI always tells me to get rid of stuff but I just can't. I don't like it. I have a lot more in storage, in an archive.

So how much have you gotten rid of?

I got rid of quite a lot of tat. I got rid of a lot of shirts because they were all dirty. They had so much make-up all over the collar – all sorts of irremovable grime. You know when you wash a shirt too much and then you get sweat marks and all that stuff?

The bane of my life.

They weren't really important shirts, maybe PRIMARK or vintage ones, or old ones that we'd made and there was just no saving them. There were also lots of T-shirts that I just accumulated over time. There's not really a lot you can do with those. Whereas coats and jackets and things like that I always think have so much more potential.

Why?

Because of the nature of how they are constructed: there are more elements to them, there are more ingredients, there's more fabric and they have more presence. There's a lot more for me to explore. Especially with gentleman's coats, there's a lot more symbolism and structure to them that you can then subvert a little bit – same with tailoring.

How much vintage do you buy?

I get a clothing budget every season. I pay myself 500 quid and use a lot of what I find for primary research.

What kind of things do you look for?

I like military wear a lot. I like uniforms. My dad was in the army, so I've always liked military clothes. I like knitwear. I rarely buy designer vintage because it's not as cost effective. The design for our bestselling jumper this season started from an Argyle knit that I bought in Aberdeen for about 50p.

Do you wear these clothes yourself? Or are they for research only?

A bit of both. Some things are more of an investment and I'll keep them in my personal wardrobe. With others, I know straight away that I'll be cutting them up or there's just a single detail or technique or fabrication that I'm interested in.

Where do you go shopping? Do you have any good tips?

I could really do with widening my net a bit more! Scotland is where I get a lot of my stuff because it's a lot cheaper and a lot of strange, interesting things wind up there, waiting to be discovered. Like this jacket – I got this in Glasgow.

That's nice. Could you describe it?

It's a tonal brown suede jacket. You can try it on if you like.

I'd love to. I'm just going to take off my jumper because I'm boiling.

Of course, do what you need to do. There's a mirror over there when you're ready. It's a super jacket, really slimming. Glasgow's the best place for '70s vintage.

This is great – huge lapels. I like that the zip stops short so it doesn't fasten all the way.

That's a nice detail. You can see your belt, which is good. I like your T-shirt.

Thank you. I got it at a FALL gig.

I fucking love THE FALL. I want to do a night called Bombast, after the song. There's no good gay indie nights that I can think of.

I really like what MARK E. SMITH is wearing on this T-shirt: a cropped Argyle sweater and an open shirt.

You could totally pull that look off. There's one image of him where he's on a bed and he has on a white shirt, black trousers and red socks. Do you know it?

I don't.

He looks so fit. Young MARK E. SMITH was totally fit.

What's that tartan you've got pinned up next to you?

This is our LOVERBOY tartan. It's registered now.

Like an actual clan tartan?

Yes! You have to apply to the tartan registry and then you have to pay them a bit of money and then they'll approve it. There are people who are tartan collectors, who are like stamp collectors, and they now message me asking for snippets. It's funny.

You're quite a fan of kilts and skirts for men, aren't you? I remember the first show of yours that I saw was the final one you did as part of MAN [Autumn and Winter 2017], and there was this guy in a double-breasted blazer and a tiny little skirt. It was such a good look: a formal mini-skirt for men.

We're doing one again this season. I want it to be really quite high up so you can just see the bulge. I think there's something really sexy about that. Guys have fucking great legs, and the funny thing I found out recently is that in adverts for tights, nine times out of ten you're looking at men's legs not women's legs.

I didn't know that.

They just have better shape. I think men really don't show off their legs enough. Mini-skirts for men are always done in a bit of an "out there", comedic way, but that suit with a skirt was quite nice.

It actually looked believable as something that a serious man in a double-breasted blazer might wear.

I would like it if eventually there's a middle-ground where male mini-skirts can be digested by the mass market. For the time being, we've got kilts. I definitely feel at my most attractive in a kilt.

Do you take good care of your clothes?

I'm starting to. I used to just come home and throw everything on the floor, but since doing my clear-out I've got much more of a routine. I take them off, fold them up or hang them in their designated space. I always make my bed before I leave, too. I never used to do that. I don't know if it's because I'm sober.

When did you stop drinking?

Earlier this year. Then I fell off the wagon a bit in the summer, but I've been sober for ten weeks. Everything just falls into place a lot easier.

Does that make you feel good, making your bed? It makes me feel good.

I love coming home to a made bed. It's just feeling like you are looking after yourself. In the past I was so much more about putting on a show, and because of the way my life and label took off: starting a club night then turning that into a label. It was all about being "The Loverboy".

You had to embody a character.

Yes, and that's fine. I'm glad I did it. I had a lot of fun and I really did enjoy myself, but I really wasn't myself for quite a while.

Was that reflected in the clear-out? Have you kept certain things while other things that were more "Loverboy" have gone?

They're still there, but they are folded away.

Talk me through what you're wearing today.

I'll start from the bottom. So, these are Dr. MARTENS, but from a YOHJI YAMAMOTO collection. I was going to wear my platforms but I really couldn't be arsed. Then I've got these big, stripy socks on. I always pull them up as high as they can go. And then I've got my Spring Summer '19 navy and white polka-dot-print trousers. Then a LOVERBOY jumper.

Which is tucked in.

But only at the front.

What's that called? A French tuck?

Is that what that is called?

I've got no idea.

Did you just make that up?

I think someone said that to me once, but I have no idea, really.

A French tuck. I'm going to use that! I'm definitely going to use that at my next show. Okay, then under my jumper I've got on a COMME shirt, which is nice and worn in. I was debating whether or not to get rid of it because it's so worn.

I quite appreciate that in a cotton shirt, when it's almost papery.

I'm into that. I'm also wearing a little red bandana scarf that I got from my friend NIALL. And then a little black beret and some jewellery. This silver band is something my grandmother gave me. My mum and my grandparents lived in Liberia, in West Africa, for 18 years. I think it's meant to ward off evil.

Very useful.

Yes, although I have to take it off when I'm drawing because it digs into my hand.

You also have a beard at the moment. Which is quite impressive. How long did that take to grow?

I get a five o'clock shadow incredibly quickly. If I shaved this morning, I would have stubble by now and it's only the early afternoon. I really like having a beard. I've definitely been getting more male attention since having it. Do you ever grow a beard?

I'm incapable of growing one. My facial hair just grows in a patchy mess, so I shave every other day to keep things neat.

Well, some people have it and some people don't. It suits you though, being clean shaven. And you have nice hair.

Thank you. I've got very hairy legs, if that counts for anything. Want to see? [Rolls up trouser leg]

Oh wow, very nice. Do you have a hairy chest as well?

I do not. Just the legs. Do you have any tattoos?

Yeah, Jupiter.

The planet?

On my chest, look. [Pulls down the neck of his jumper]

It's massive. Is that your astrological planet?

No, I was just obsessed with Jupiter as a kid. I often say it's because it's the ruling planet for Sagittarius – my mum's sign – but really it's just because I like it. It's beautiful, it's stunning, and it's one of the reasons we're not being pummelled by asteroids.

You run a lot now, don't you?

Yeah, I go running a lot. I went this morning. I love it. I'm looking slim.

You're looking good.

People have commented on it recently. I run as much as possible. It's such a nice, cathartic thing. I'm not going out dancing as much, I'm not going clubbing, so that's a good way to engage with music. I'm actually running the 2019 London Marathon.

Incredible. Who are you doing it for?

Dementia Revolution. Look, here's my official top. I've not worn it yet, but it says "Loverboy" on it. I need to practise running in it so I don't get nipple chafe. I said I'd raise ten grand for them and I'm a bit worried I can't.

You can do it. One thing I love about sports is that it opens up new opportunities for dressing up. What do you wear when you go running?

I've got a LES BOYS LES GIRLS thing that they sent me. It's a weird two-piece jogging bottoms and sweater which works, but I ran today in shorts. I haven't really gotten into trying on lots of sports stuff yet.

It's one of my favourite things.

Maybe I should. What sports do you do?

I run and I play football.

What's your go-to brand for football?

It depends on what team I'm playing for. But if I'm wearing whatever I want, I wear dark blue NIKE shorts. I bought some amazing boots from ADIDAS recently that are silver and blue – they look like space boots. And I've got a lot of Italian national team shirts, which are a nice colour of blue.

Are you Italian?

A little bit.

I can tell – it's the brows.

Are they a giveaway?

And your legs, too! I'm going to dress up more with my sports clothing.

You should. Good running kit, a flattering top. It can feel quite powerful dressing up that way, and especially coming back from a run.

Oh my god, I feel so empowered when I come off a run. I'm red and sweating and people are, like, "He's done something." People can feel the energy radiating off you. I fucking love it.

Can I ask why your family lived in Liberia for so long?

My granddad was a railway safety engineer, an incredible man, and he was helping to build this railway that was going across west Africa. My mum lived there intermittently, so she was there for 18 years but got schooling in Scotland. They lived in this community that was a bit shut off from the world; it was full of Swedish workers who were also working on the railway.

It sounds like an incredible life.

That style of living also crept into my life as well, with my dad being in the army, because in army housing, everyone lives in the same type of houses. All dads do the same thing. Then you have the army-wives thing. When my mum and dad divorced, we went to live in a council estate in Scotland... Sorry, I don't know where this is going.

It's fine. You've mentioned your dad a couple of times and his being in the military. In terms of your interest in clothes it seems like a bit of a reference point for you.

It's funny, because, if you think about it, I'm a very colourful, gay version of what he would look like: military boots, military beret. He has always been into his appearance. He's very much into his looks but in a "doesn't like to admit it" kind of way. I have a lot of memories of him shining his shoes or steaming his beret.

You have to steam berets?

Yeah to make them really perfect. He was a very attractive man, my dad. My mum as well. Fucking hell, my mum is stunning. They were a really gorgeous couple.

Do you want to talk about some other style influences?

I talk about this all the time, but really, it's THE HORRORS. That was the first time, as a teen in Scotland, that I thought, "I just want to look exactly like this." I've never wanted to look more like anything, ever: the skinniest jeans, pointy winkle-picker shoes or Chelsea boots with a curved heel, and massive hair. It allowed me to channel being gay, but in some ways it was safer, because it was ambiguous. My first and only boyfriend, who is no longer my boyfriend, was very much that. It's sort of my taste.

It's interesting that you are so influenced by them, because their look was essentially HEDI SLIMANE at DIOR, and that aesthetic doesn't really show in your work.

The thing is, when the new CELINE came out, I fucking loved it. I'll always love that look. That's the look I'm attracted to; that's what I want my future boyfriend to look like. That's my thing; that's what I'm really attracted to.

And yet the return of that aesthetic drew some criticism for perhaps not being representative enough of what people want or need now. Whereas you are championed as being this figurehead of a new way of dressing.

It's funny that it doesn't really show in my work. I see it as being somewhat separate – that sort of restrictiveness. If I was suddenly to get another house to do, then that would be fun as a fresh start.

Is taking over at a house something that you are interested in?

Oh yeah, massively. I'd love to.

What's your dream house?

I don't know if I'm allowed to say.

Because you are in conversations with somewhere?

I can't say anything.

That in itself is quite interesting.

Obviously there are things I want to master here, there's lots of stuff that needs to be tied up, and it's a small business we need to make as much effort as possible to make sure we keep ourselves afloat, that staff are paid on time, that we hit targets. But I don't see myself only doing LOVERBOY for ten years.

And do you think you'll keep showing in London, and keep showing during men's? Or do you ever think about switching?

I would never want to feel that I was abandoning London. But I don't know – I love doing womenswear now and I would never want to feel too restricted. If you look at our market, the majority of it is younger women and then a strong clientele of more mature women. That's the thing about LOVERBOY. You can say it's this or it's that, but to me it's very amorphous. I mean, it started as a club night and now it's a label.

(Ends)

(continued from p. 37) who's, like, "I'm super inspired by DAVID BOWIE." I wouldn't want to copy style like that because our bodies are very different. I'm a big boy. I'm tall and have some shape to me. It's quite easy to be elegant when you are tall and skinny, but it took time for me to learn how my own body could be elegant. I think I learnt that big boys could be elegant through seeing people like JULIAN SCHNABEL. Although, I'm smaller, I must say.

Can you describe the state of your closet? Is it tidy, messy, super organised and are your clothes folded, boxed, grouped by colour or season, etcetera?

It's messy because I have too many clothes; I buy lots of clothes from the designers I represent. I have lots of SACAI, lots of LEMAIRE, more commercial JW ANDERSON pieces. Outside of my clients, I think I only buy RALPH LAUREN – it's good for my body. To free up space I have been sending my old clothes to the south of France. That way I don't have to take any luggage when I travel there and I can rediscover all the old clothes that I might not wear in Paris.

Have you ever made a radical change to your "look"?

No, but right now I think I'm too boring. I'm 42 and I feel that I need to evolve my style. I'm wearing classic clothes and I look like a classic middle-aged guy rather than someone dressed up like that. It was good when I was younger but now I'm the proper age of the people who actually wear these things. Suddenly I'm in a uniform. I don't like being so literal; I like to surprise people.

So you don't like uniforms then?

Oh no, I love a uniform. I love a pair of jeans, sneakers and navy-blue jumpers from A.P.C. It's a very good uniform for me. But then I like to throw it off with certain things. Maybe it's the shoes, or the shirt, or a certain LOEWE bag that makes me look a bit like a rich woman.

What do you wear to look and feel sexy?

I wear a classic shirt with jeans. It makes me look like a daddy, I think people like that.

JOHAN KUGELBERG and the most unbelievable cotton

A questionnaire from December 2016 with a Swedish archivist and curator. Johan runs the Boo-Hooray archive in his adopted hometown of New York City.

What garment is key to your personal style?

Whether it's T-shirts, jeans, shirts or sweaters, anything made of the most unbelievable cotton.

How many things made of unbelievable cotton do you have in your wardrobe?

Hundreds.

What is it specifically about garments made from cotton that you love?

The feel of it against the skin. These are items worn purely for one's own enjoyment and comfort rather than how they look. I increasingly buy garments based largely on how they feel.

What are the defining specifications for the most unbelievable cotton?

It's like a binary code and when you touch it you just know, yes or no. Cotton often becomes unbelievable after it has aged. I have jeans that I have owned for 15 to 20 years and the cotton is only just starting to become unbelievable. Similarly, you can get newer garments that are unbelievable. J.CREW has really amazing cotton. Right now, I am wearing two items made from unbelievable cotton. One is a new sweater by AGNÈS B. that is thick and slightly coarse – I felt it in the shop and bought three straight away. Underneath that is a 25-year-old PAUL SMITH shirt; it's more starched and stiff but also incredibly smooth. So, there aren't any rules. I think it is definitely a Proustian thing: it's specific to each person and how it makes them feel. Just as foods and smells trigger personal memory, so does the tactility of clothing. I think that is something to be indulged.

Do you know where your attachment to this kind of cotton comes from? How did this come about, do you think?

It's probably from my dad. Both my dad and my grandfather were really athletic. My grandfather was a sprinter in the 1932 Olympics and ADI DASSLER was best man at his wedding. My father did decathlon in the military and was an acquaintance of RENÉ LACOSTE. So through these strange connections to sporting dynasties, I grew up with loads of vintage sportswear. I wore castaways and second-hand items like sweaters and polos. They were made of the most unbelievable cotton. These are the kind of items you will see sold for exorbitant prices in vintage menswear stores in Tokyo and Osaka, because the cut and the fabric are something else. A tip for spotting old LACOSTE is that the crocodile logo has LACOSTE written in cursive script on the body. If you find anything with that logo, buy it. It will blow your mind.

Do you think you are alone in your obsession for cotton?

Through my work I spend a lot of time setting up archives and working closely with groups from very specific subcultures, and I always end up talking to them about clothes and my cotton obsession. When I was setting up the Cornell Hip Hop Collection, which is the biggest archive in the world devoted to the history of hip hop, I spent five to ten years hanging out with hip-hop legends, which was really wonderful. All they ever talk about is men's clothing. They're obsessed. They don't talk about other MCs, they don't talk about women, and they don't talk about music. They just talk about clothes.

Have you ever been tempted to get rid of all your clothes and start again from scratch?

Not so much. However, I have lost a lot of the clothing that I once owned. I had big collections of punk T-shirts that have gone into the punk archives I made for Cornell University and Yale, because the punk T-shirt is such an important part of the punk narrative. But I have kept hold of an original 'Punk Magazine' T-shirt from around 1976 or 1977 – of course the cotton is unbelievable. It's starting to crumble a bit, but then again so am I.

What amazing tip for wardrobe maintenance can you share?

Don't be afraid of lavender. I know lots of people think it smells slightly grannyish, but it doesn't. Putting some in your wardrobe and drawers will keep your clothes smelling fresh and keep moths away. You just have to make sure to change it regularly.

ABDO HUSSEIN and his boring political suit

A questionnaire from May 2018 with a Dutchman in London. Abdo moved to the UK from the city of Eindhoven and is a case officer at a healthcare charity.

What garment is key to your personal style?

I wouldn't say it's key to my personal style specifically, but I have an unspectacular dark blue suit that's been important for me.

What is it specifically about this unspectacular suit that you love?

I work for a healthcare charity that helps hospitals, so a lot of my job involves meeting with Members of Parliament and convincing them to do things. Before that I worked as a staffer for an MP. I've found this boring suit is helpful for interacting with politicians.

Why's that?

Clothes in politics are funny. It's all about fitting in and knowing your place. When you work for an MP you should always be in the background; the emphasis should never be on you. So, wearing the most boring, forgettable suit possible is important. It's like camouflage. I've carried that logic over into my current job, too. I don't wear my suit as often, but I know how politicians think and I know the importance of not standing out too much. In a weird kind of way, you try to mirror them. When you're trying to pressure or persuade politicians to take up certain policies, you're trying to make them feel comfortable, almost so they start thinking, "Oh I'm with one of my staffers." I want to be part of the furniture. Making them feel comfortable means that they will be more likely to remember whatever I say. I know that as soon as you start impressing them or you come across as too slick, they'll get distracted and stop listening to you.

What are the defining specifications of your unspectacular suit?

It's just the most normal-looking suit in the world, and that's the point. It's dark blue, made of some sort of wool-blend. I got it from a shop in Manchester that I can't actually remember the name of. It's so inoffensive. I could just walk down the street and be any other guy.

So, if staffers have to be almost invisible, does this mean that as you progress up the political ladder you get to wear more exciting clothes?

Yeah, you do. Well, relatively exciting. Suits get a little more fitted; you can look a little sharper. Then among the MPs you also have a difference between backbenchers and frontbenchers. The optics are very much focused on those in the front row of the House of Commons, so they often look better put together. Whereas backbenchers can get away with a little more: they can look a little scruffier or you might catch one of them wearing a pink shirt. But there's always a balance in politics. Even if you're a frontbench MP, you can't be too sharply dressed.

That's interesting. It does seem as though politicians always have to strike this fine balance between looking impressive but not looking too impressive. They need to look as palatable as possible.

There's definitely a balancing act. If the voters see someone who is too slick of suit, they could come to resent them: "This guy doesn't know my pain! What does he know about real life in his slick suit?" Whereas if someone is wearing something more normal and relatable they might look and think: "This guy gets me." However, a politician shouldn't make the mistake of looking too normal or unassuming. Voters also need to feel inspired by someone. They need to feel that this is a person who can represent their constituency and their country. Like so much in politics, you need to strike a middle ground. It's a tension between not looking too good and not looking too bad. I think JEREMY CORBYN is a perfect example. Since becoming leader of the Labour Party, his suits have become a lot sharper and he is seen wearing ties more often. His demographic has expanded from just Islington North and he has toned down the scruffy, liberal metropolitan vibe and made himself more appealing to a wider range of people. Also, just look at THERESA MAY. She often gets negative press for her appearance but it's tough for her. She's not some businesswoman who is dressing to impress a board of investors. She has to dress to be appealing to 60 million people across a huge range of demographics and in a way that won't alienate anyone.

Is it true that politicians dress differently depending on their party?

Oh yes. There's still a lot of tribalism. In general, politicians tend to dress quite similarly but there are some tell-tale differences. Tories are more likely to wear bespoke suits and they tend to wear ties more often; they'll keep them on even when they're not in the House of Commons. A Labour politician would never wear a double-breasted suit because of the class connotations, whereas for someone like JACOB REES-MOGG, his double-breasted suit is a huge part of his personal brand. He is saying: "I can be your leader and fight off these EU tyrants and preserve good old-fashioned Britishness. Just look at my suit!" Also, Tories tend to wear cufflinks, while Labour MPs have button cuffs.

I had no idea about the cufflinks. Are pinstripes a Conservative thing too?

Oh no, no, no, no, no. Not even Tories would wear pinstripes. It's too private sector.

Describe your wardrobe. What else do you have in there?

I've got a lot of white T-shirts. A lot of black jeans. Three or four pairs of NIKE Air Max in plain colourways. And my one boring navy suit. I'm really quite a casually dressed guy. I find wearing a suit is a little bit like wearing a costume.

Does that make wearing the suit a bit fun, or even a bit sexy?

You are totally right. It does feel like that because I so rarely wear it.

Where do you get your work shirts from?

Either COS or UNIQLO.

French cuffs or button cuffs?

Oh button cuffs, of course!

BONNE REIJN and his Bonne Suit

A questionnaire from October 2016 with the Dutch designer and stylist. Bonne is the creative mind behind Bonne Suits and co-founded the Amsterdam shop Zeedijk 60.

What garment is key to your personal style?

A workwear suit of my own invention, called a Bonne Suit. It's a practical garment in which you can do whatever you want, whenever you want.

How many Bonne Suits do you have in your wardrobe?

I have lots.

What is it specifically about your suits that you love?

The suits are directly inspired by farmers' overalls, which are made from heavy cotton so they don't get destroyed easily. ISSEY MIYAKE's suits are another big inspiration; they are in between a tailored suit and a pyjama. So my suits are sturdy and relaxed while looking tailored and sharp. Most importantly, I can put them in the washing machine and get my pasta sauce stains out.

Is your dress style something from your youth, or something you picked up from a specific person?

I started wearing farmers' overalls as soon as I could walk. I used to spend my summers in Dedemsvaart with my mother and my great aunt MIEN RUYS, the landscape architect. We'd live there in her big gardens and the only time I wasn't playing outside was when I was sleeping, so I'd get dirty a lot. The overalls were the perfect solution to keeping my clothes clean.

What defines your style of dressing?

I'm constantly caught between looking like a bum and trying to look like the late Prince BERNHARD of the Netherlands. I'm also usually covered in sauce stains because I'm always making pasta.

Who else do you typically look at for style inspiration?

My mother and, later on, my foster mother are really my only sources of inspiration for how people should dress.

Can you describe the state of your closet? Is it tidy, messy, super organised and are your clothes folded, boxed, grouped by season or colour, etcetera?

It's super messy. I lose clothing all the time. I am trying to become more of a balanced, organised person but I don't think it will ever happen.

Do you pick out what you're going to wear the night before?

I usually just have to go with whatever is cleanest.

Is there a garment that you used to dislike but ended up loving and wearing?

No, I don't really think about clothing in that way.

Have you ever made a radical change in your "look"? Have you ever been tempted to get rid of all your clothes and start again from scratch?

Not really. Between the ages of 12 and 18 I would only wear one outfit. I thought I was a mod so I'd only wear FRED PERRY polos and I had one pair of wide pants. I seriously only had one pair of pants. Then I suddenly discovered fashion and I started wearing RICK OWENS and DAMIR DOMA, but I realised quite soon that my farmer's body just wasn't made for this beautiful skinny silhouette and gradually my idea for the BONNE SUITS came along.

Do you think having a strict uniform is a relief or do you consider it a loss of options?

I do consider it a loss of options, and what a relief!

What do you wear to look sexy? Do you have a pick-up look?

I've had steady girlfriends since the tender age of 13, so I've never actually picked up a girl before! But I love to look sexy for myself. I feel sexy in my own suits or my ISSEY MIYAKE suit.

SAM ASHBY and his Blundstone boots

A questionnaire from December 2016 with the British filmmaker. Sam directed the fantastic short film, 'The Colour of His Hair', starring Josh O'Connor.

What garment is key to your personal style?

A pair of black BLUNDSTONE Super 550 boots.

How many pairs of these boots do you have in your wardrobe?

Just the one. I wear them until they are beyond repair and then I replace them. My previous pair lasted for about two years before finally perishing in the New Hampshire snow in January.

What is it specifically about BLUNDSTONE's boots that you love?

To me, they are the perfect boot. Most of BLUNDSTONE's boots are hideous, but a simple pair of black 500s or 550s look great and don't take much looking after. They also serve me well in the city and the countryside, which at the moment is key as I'm travelling between the two a lot. You can pull them on and kick them off with ease, which appeals to my lazy side and is ideal for airport security.

Do you know where your attachment to this garment comes from? Is it something from your youth, or something you picked up from a specific person?

I was at a film festival in Germany a few years ago and met a girl who was wearing the most amazing pair of boots. I told her how much I loved them, and asked her what make they were. I eventually tracked them down at the Natural Shoe Store, a wonderfully uncool establishment in London's Covent Garden.

How do you feel when you see others wearing the same thing? Are you happy to have the whole world wear "your" garment or do you prefer to stand out?

Since I "borrowed" them from someone else, it doesn't bother me at all. I just feel a little surge of admiration for them and their excellent taste in footwear.

Who or what do you look at for style inspiration? Do you look at fashion?

I like to look at films for style inspiration. My biggest style influence to date is probably WINONA RYDER, especially in 'Reality Bites', for her blue denim, pocket T-shirts and tortoiseshell sunglasses, which I wore pretty consistently throughout my twenties. 'Gamins de Paris', a porn film by JEAN-DANIEL CADINOT set in 1945, also had a direct influence on my wardrobe. The boys in it wear a combination of cotton shorts, black boots and white thick wool socks that became a recent summer staple.

Can you describe the state of your closet?

My wardrobe has been getting progressively smaller, especially since the move from London to Yorkshire and Amsterdam. I've basically narrowed it down to one pair of trousers, one pair of jeans, a handful of

T-shirts, one shirt, two sweaters, and two jackets. It's mostly black, with a hint of electric blue, racing-green or white, here and there. It barely takes up half a rail, and so is very easy to manage.

Is there a garment that you used to dislike but ended up loving and wearing?

I never buy things that I dislike, but sometimes I buy things that are simply too weird or difficult to wear. For example, I have a pair of what I can only describe as "hairy" shorts by SEBASTIAAN PIETER GROENEN's brilliant label PIETER that I bought at one of his sample sales. They are a marvellous one-off, complete with what looks like a silver cock ring hanging from a loop at the waist. Funnily enough I have yet to find the right moment to wear them, but I'm keeping my fingers crossed.

Have you ever made a radical change in your "look"?

I usually wear things until I get bored of them, but I think my current "look", or non-look as it should probably be called, is faring rather better than previous looks, maybe because it's so basic. I have stripped away so much that it does feel a little like starting from scratch, actually.

Do you have a dress code for work?

I'm self-employed and much of my work is done at a desk, so I have no division between daywear and workwear. At the moment it's basically all black, all the time. This has to change.

What do you wear to look sexy?

In summer it's shorts, without a doubt. I was so shy about my legs as a teenager that I'd wear jeans to the beach, but now I'll get them out at any opportunity. I think winter is the sexiest season, though. I love stripping down to longjohns and a pair of thick wool socks in front of the fire at home in Yorkshire.

What amazing tip for wardrobe management can you share?

I'm an editor at heart. It applies to my wardrobe too.

CHARLIE FAITH and the Hawaiian shirt

A questionnaire from August 2017 with the writer, actor and TV producer. Charlie lives in Los Angeles.

What garment is key to your personal style?

The Hawaiian shirt.

How many Hawaiian shirts do you have in your wardrobe?

God, hard to say. I collect them. I've got probably close to 20 in total but there are six or seven that make up my main rotation, including two or three vintage shirts from the '60s and '70s.

What is it specifically about this garment that you love?

If you wear one to the office, there's no question you're peacocking. But hey, Hawaiian shirts are designed to be worn while you're getting drunk on a beach. Who doesn't want that vibe to be their day-to-day?

What are the defining specifications that make the perfect Hawaiian shirt?

There have been a lot of great examples and styles throughout the decades. There's the coked-out parrot shirts of the '80s, the giant collars from the '70s...

Do you know where your attachment to these shirts comes from? Is it something from your youth, or something you picked up from a specific person? When, who?

It was kind of a perfect storm. I went to a Catholic school and had to wear a uniform. However, on Fridays we could wear whatever we wanted as long as the shirt had a collar. Wearing something flamboyant seemed like the perfect troll on the forced drabness of Catholicism. Also, my dad's buddy had been collecting them since the '60s, so quality shirts were never in short supply.

How do you feel when you see other men

wearing Hawaiian shirts? Are you happy to have the whole world wear "your" garment or do you prefer to stand out?

Probably the most popular version of the Hawaiian shirt right now is the muted trash they sell to old white men at TOMMY BAHAMA. The beige Hawaiian shirt is the coward's Hawaiian shirt. That said, living in Los Angeles, you see a lot of people wearing real ones – we always acknowledge each other while grabbing a round of drinks at the bar.

Can you describe the state of your closet? Is it tidy, messy, super organised and are your clothes folded, boxed, grouped by colour or season, etcetera?

It's bad. Total disorganised disaster. I do try to keep all my Hawaiian shirts clumped together right in the middle though.

Is there a garment that you used to dislike but ended up loving and wearing?

I'm going through a pretty serious sweatshirt renaissance right now. I used to hate them because they made me feel like I was wearing the gross sweat suits they would issue us for gym class in school, but there's something simple and cool about them if worn right. More Catholic trauma I guess.

Have you ever been tempted to get rid of all your clothes and start again from scratch?

I could never ditch my whole closet. I do a lot of sketch comedy and I'd be traumatised to let go of my costumes and wigs.

Have you ever considered settling on a strict uniform and if so, what would it be? Would you consider it a relief, or a loss of options?

After nine years of Catholic school, I have had my fill of that. It took me a long time to figure out what the fuck I even liked to wear when I got to college. I had never had to think about it before.

What do you wear to look sexy? Do you have a pick-up look?

In my experience, the best thing a guy can do is try to look like you didn't think about what you're wearing at all. A lot of guys want to be the best-dressed guy in the room, but no one wants to talk to the guy wearing a suit at a dive bar.

What amazing tip for wardrobe or maintenance can you share?

I'm terrible at this. I know that I only wear 25 per cent of my wardrobe. Can you send someone to come collect the other 75 per cent? It's too emotionally difficult for me.

GEORGE RAYNER-LAW and his Dutch overalls

A questionnaire from November 2017 with an audio-visual technician. George is from London and works at the Tate Modern gallery.

What garment is key to your personal style?

Overalls – Dutch military surplus, purchased from eBay circa 2012 (£8 + postage).

How many of these overalls do you have in your wardrobe?

One.

What is it specifically about this garment that you love?

If I'm comparing them to others of the form: the epaulettes, the fact that they don't taper in at the waist and that I can fit my arms halfway into the pockets.

What are the defining specifications that make the perfect overalls?

They should be loose and have a breeze. I also enjoy the sense of the garment hanging entirely on the shoulders; as someone who doesn't often wear dresses or robes, this is a novel feeling.

Do you know where your attachment to this garment comes from? Is it something from your youth, or something you picked up from a specific person? When, who?

There was a time in my life where they felt vital. I was feeling very dissociated and wearing something that obviously made me stand out on the street helped to confirm my existence. During this same period a close friend of mine passed away and the dress code for his funeral was "Wear what you feel fabulous in," so I wore my overalls under a black V-neck pullover. I couldn't have gone in anything else.

How do you feel when you see other men wearing the same thing? Are you happy to have the whole world wear "your" garment or do you prefer to stand out?

It's rare to see people in big green overalls outside certain working environments. The cut of mine is also very different to most others. If I saw someone wearing "my" overalls, I would feel, I think, threatened.

Who or what do you look at for style inspiration? Do you look at fashion?

One of my earliest style inspirations was IAN CURTIS, because he's one of the few very tall men in culture who also managed to dress well. Regarding my overalls, a key inspiration was RODCHENKO and the idea of artists as cultural engineers. I don't really follow fashion. Primarily, I get my clothes from charity shops.

Can you describe the state of your closet? Is it tidy, messy, super organised?

I have limited space: half a clothes rail shared with my girlfriend, classic IKEA hanging drawers with neatly folded contents, shirts and jackets hanging up, and an overflowing laundry basket.

Have you ever made a radical change in your "look"? Have you ever been tempted to start again from scratch?

I once got rid of all my denim and now I only wear trousers. I also no longer buy T-shirts and I would say they are gradually getting phased out of my wardrobe. In particular I avoid wearing T-shirts with anything related to music or politics on them – the last thing I want is to get stuck in a conversation about something I'm wearing.

Have you ever considered settling on a strict uniform and if so, what would it be? Would you consider it a relief, or a loss of options?

From the age of 18 I made a conscious decision to only ever own one set of footwear at a time. I started with 10-eyelet DR. MARTENS boots and currently I have an 11-eyelet pair by SOLOVAIR. I wax them regularly and polish them when I need to look smart. I replace them when they are just about to collapse; my last pair had full splits along both soles before I got new ones. I have sometimes considered extending this principal to the rest of my wardrobe as I find freedom from choice helpful in allowing me to get on with all the other things I want to do.

What do you wear to look sexy? Do you have a pick-up look?

Not as such, but a definite go to would be my beetle-green YVES SAINT LAURENT shirt which I bought for £7.50 from a high-street charity shop.

What amazing tip for wardrobe management or maintenance can you share?

Actively police your socks. You almost certainly have too many.

CESAR PADILLA and the vintage dress shirt

A questionnaire from May 2017 with the fashion archivist and curator. Cesar runs the popular New York City vintage clothing enterprise Cherry and sings and plays guitar.

What garment is key to your personal style?

Vintage cotton dress shirts.

How many vintage cotton dress shirts do you have in your wardrobe?

A hundred.

What is it specifically about these old cotton dress shirts that you love?

I love the feel of old cotton – so much so, I even sleep in my vintage dress shirts. There is rarely anything sexier than a man in a dress shirt and a pair of tightie-whities.

Do you know where your attachment to

them comes from? Is it something from your youth, or something you picked up from a specific person?

It really comes from four BROOKS BROTHERS shirts I found in a bachelor's cottage on the North Shore of Long Island about ten years ago. I tried one on and that was that. I immediately understood the power of their simplicity and masculinity. I decided that day that it was time I dressed up every day. My father also wore a dress shirt or a white cotton T-shirt almost every day. He had come to the United States from Mexico in the late 1940s and worked at various race tracks in the Southern California/Baja California area, and he was often the handler for many winning horses. There were tons of photos of my well-dressed father holding the reigns of many horses, next to their gleaming prize winning owners. As I looked through these photographs I realised that I definitely had adopted some of my father's style. Most importantly, I realised I had my father's body.

How do you feel when you see other men wearing the same thing?

I work on a lot of period films with their costume designers, and many actors wear my personal clothing in them. For example, RUSSELL CROWE wears my 1970s LEVI'S throughout the entire film 'American Gangster'. RYAN GOSLING also wears my Monster Trucks T-shirt inside-out in the film 'The Place Beyond the Pines'. I purchased this T-shirt while dosing on LSD in New Orleans in 1991, the night of the infamous gubernatorial race between EDWIN EDWARDS, BUDDY ROEMER and DAVID DUKE (the former head of the KKK). All the BEACH BOYS also wear articles of clothing from my closet in the recent film 'Love and Mercy'. In this respect, I have no problem seeing my personal clothing on another man.

Do you look at fashion?

I don't pay attention to contemporary fashion whatsoever. I find it very boring for the most part.

What do you wear to look sexy?

I have a saying: "If you don't feel sexy walking out the door then don't walk out the door." In other words, all my clothes are sexy. I also don't own a mirror, so all my clothes have to work no matter what. It makes it so much easier not having to look at yourself before you go out the door. You go with your gut, or at least I do.

What amazing tip for wardrobe management or maintenance can you share?

The best advice I can give is to not care. If it's stained then toss it. Wrinkles – who cares? If you look good, you look good. There's not enough starch in the world to change that.

What ultimately signifies your style of dressing?

Fun. I live for fun.

GRAYSON PERRY and his flouncy dresses

A questionnaire from July 2017 with the artist. Grayson is famous for his ceramics and tapestries, and has an alter-ego called Claire.

What garment is key to your personal style?

I suppose in the public imagination I'm wearing a flouncy little-girl dress. Once you've popped your head over the parapet, the public and the media will glue whatever you're wearing at that moment onto your body and that will remain fixed. So in the public and the media's imagination I'm defined conceptually by a flouncy little-girl dress. I call it the crack-cocaine of femininity.

Crack-cocaine? Is there something addictive about flouncy little-girl dresses?

There is if you're a transvestite. Probably not for many other people.

How many little-girl dresses do you have in your wardrobe?

I probably have a dozen out of the almost 200 dresses that I have in my wardrobe. They form a relatively small part of my dress collection, in which I've got everything from relatively modest ones where women go, "Ooh I'd like that dress," right through to looking like a clown from outer space.

What is it specifically about little-girl dresses that you love?

It's because I'm a transvestite and they turn me on. It's just the symbolism of it and how it's the furthest thing away from macho-functional clothing. It's all about being pretty and silly and frilly and vulnerable and innocent. Rather than the opposite, which is the guy in his combat fatigues and his tattoos. A lot of transvestites like to dress up as women from the high street and fit in, and I do that sometimes. It's kind of interesting but nobody pays you any attention; you're just another slightly tall woman walking about. That doesn't really tick many boxes for me. If I'm wearing a dress, I want to access a certain sort of attention. There's something fetishistic about it. It's like when a guy puts on a leather jacket: somewhere deep in his mind he wants to feel that he's being regarded as a rufty-tufty biker.

You like to feel confident that people are looking at you as a man in a dress rather than thinking you might be a woman?

Exactly. I'm unmistakably a man in a little-girl dress, or whatever dress I'm wearing. I'm not deceiving anyone. That's an aspect of transvestism that I have sort of struggled with, this idea that I'm pulling the wool over people's eyes and then they get a surprise when you open your mouth in a shop. I make sure anybody, even from a passing helicopter, can spot that I am a man in a dress.

What are the defining specifications that make the perfect little-girl dress?

It should have puffy sleeves, a sticky-outy skirt (like the classic toilet-door symbol shape), a high waist, a PETER PAN collar, probably a bit of frill or lace on it and flowers or hearts or something – all the clichés of doll dresses. I have all my dresses made for me and I usually ask my students to make them. I've been working with students for 13 years, and I know exactly what to ask for in terms of the cut and silhouette that work with my body, which is basically that my chest, waist and hips are exactly the same.

Do you know where your attachment to this garment comes from? Is it something from your youth, or something you picked up from a specific person? When, who?

I was pretty drawn to little-girl dresses from the off, when I was about twelve. But I didn't ever feel brave enough to wear one or couldn't get one in my size. It wasn't until I was in my late thirties that I was a) brave enough to go out in one and b) had the budget to have them made.

Who or what do you look at for style inspiration? Do you look at fashion?

I look at fashion a lot. I don't like high-street fashion because it's quite dull and watered down, but couture I'm quite interested in. I usually read reviews in the papers. I like student fashion shows in particular because that's when they're at their most bonkers, before the pressure to be commercial kicks in. I like busy and colourful, you know? I've seen enough deconstructed jackets. I call it "fashionstudentitis", where everything is asymmetric and deconstructed. Yawnarama!

Can you describe the state of your closet? Is it tidy, messy, super organised?

I've got my studio, my house in the country and I've got a place in London, and I keep dresses at each place and rotate them seasonally. So when the weather changes I'll bring my thicker clothes back and store my summer clothes. I often do car journeys between the places with my car full of dresses.

Is there a garment that you used to dislike but ended up loving and wearing? When did your aversion to it turn to fondness? What changed your mind?

It's more the other way round, actually: there are lots of things that I won't buy now. I won't buy black. I refuse to buy black. It's a really tight rule with me. I call it "coward's black". It'll go with everything, you never have to make a decision and you're never going to stand out. So black I avoid. Denim I also struggle with. The only time I might wear either of those things is when I'm on my motorbike and dressing up as a biker.

What do you wear when you're dressed in male clothing?

Colour. I always buy colourful clothing. I used to go to HACKETT because they'd be good for a colourful trouser, but they've gone mellow on me. I basically live in a UNIQLO fleece, as brightly coloured a pair of trousers as possible, a coloured T-shirt, and there are some very jazzy trainers around at the moment so I've got lots of choice there. That's the uniform I wear most of the time when I'm not dressed up. It's important to understand that I'm the same person in both, whether I'm dressing in men's clothes or...other clothes. I don't think you could really call them women's clothes anyway, as it's just my clothing, made for a man, rather than designed with a woman's body in mind.

What make-up do you buy?

All sorts: CLINIQUE, MAC. I like theatrical make-up because it's a bit stronger. I'm planning to go out and buy some today, actually. I'm going to pop down to CHARLES FOX's and get some of their super-strength stuff. It's a shop in Covent Garden that sells theatrical make-up. You can get better colours there, and things like strong blushers. When I put on make-up, sometimes I go for the rosy-cheeked look if I feel it's appropriate for the occasion, and sometimes I tone it down a bit. It depends. I sometimes go for face jewels. I've got a whole drawerful of face jewels. They look like acne from more than ten yards away, which is a downside, but I still think they look great. •

CHARLIE MacLEAN and the monocle

A questionnaire from May 2018 with a 66-year-old whisky expert. Charlie lives in Edinburgh and is a Master of the Quaich, one of the most prestigious positions in the world of whisky.

What garment is key to your personal style?

The monocle.

How many monocles do you have?

I have two. One is from SPECSAVERS and the other was given to me. It used to belong to Sir ALEXANDER WALKER, grandson of the legendary JOHNNIE WALKER. It's a lovely thing with a gold frame. I really should just use it for dress purposes but I wear it all the time. Now, JOHNNIE of course used to wear a lorgnette, rather than a monocle, but nonetheless it does have this lovely connection with whisky.

What is it specifically about the monocle that you love?

Its ease of access. It is always just dangling helpfully around my neck, so I don't have to plunge around desperately trying to find my bloody spectacles when I need to read credit cards and mobile phones. I've left dozens of pairs of spectacles in restaurants and once dropped a pair into the North Sea while fixing the outboard motor of a boat, but my monocle is always just there, exactly where you need it.

So it is more of a practical object?

Yes, although it has become one of my identifying marks, I suppose. I have a string of bars named after me across China [Charles' Whisky Bars] and their logo is simply a monocle and a moustache. What was born out of practicality has become my trademark. You also cut a bit of a dash when using it to read a wine list in a restaurant.

Can you remember when your attachment to the monocle started?

A long time ago I was holidaying in Assynt, away up in the far north of Scotland, and I bust one of the lenses on my reading glasses. In a place like that, where there is no television and the weather can be particularly terrible, reading is essential! Anyway, I discovered I could read perfectly well with one lens, so I went along to SPECSAVERS the moment I got home and bought my first one; I've loved them ever since.

Would you ever pass your monocle down to someone else in the whisky game? To continue the lineage?

When I become completely doolally, or incapable of fulfilling my useful function, I will hand it on. It does take a bit of time getting used to, as it has to sort of grip into your eye socket, but luckily it fits me perfectly.

How do you feel when you see other men wearing the same thing? Are you happy to have the whole world wear a monocle or do you prefer to stand out?

I think I have only met two people, out of all the thousands of people I meet, who wear a monocle – it's a tiny club. On both occasions there has been an immediate fellow feeling, a kind of "Ooh so you've discovered the benefits too, eh?"

Do you have a dress code for work? Does your work influence what you wear?

Less and less so. Even when doing tastings or presentations there is less of an expectation to dress up, which is a shame, as it is quite fun to dress up every now and then. I'm an advocate of the light-tweed suit. I have two or three that I feel very comfortable in and they look great. One of the things that is de rigeur costume is a kilt, but they don't do too well in hot climates or air-conditioned hotels.

Is there a garment that you used to dislike but ended up loving and wearing? When did your aversion to it turn to fondness? What changed your mind?

Funnily enough I would have to say the kilt. I had to wear one as a boy to go to church on Sundays, so for I long time I only associated it with that. Bare legs on a cold pew is never an enjoyable sensation.

Have you ever considered settling on a strict uniform and if so, what would it be? Would you consider it a relief, or a loss of options?

No, certainly not. I would make the comparison with whisky, and indeed wine, that to drink the same whisky or wine everyday is pathetic! I would hate to wear the same thing all the time. Changing your costume according to mood and weather and location is good fun really. It's an essential part of life... One has to match the occasion, the situation, the mood and the carpet.

EDWIN DORLEY and the long-sleeved T-shirt

A questionnaire from September 2016 with an assistive-technology teacher living in Manchester, UK. Edwin also runs the cassette-tape label I Hate My Records.

What garment is key to your personal style?

Ultra heavy 100 per cent cotton long-sleeved crew-neck black T-shirts from GILDAN.

How many long-sleeved black GILDAN T-shirts do you have in your wardrobe?

Five.

What is it specifically about these T-shirts that you love?

They are my default tops these days. They're a garment for all occasions and climates. You can wear them under things; you can wear them over things. In the summer you can wear them on their own. They're cheap and disposable. I operate on a one-in, one-out basis: usually when a shirt becomes too irreversibly dirty it's time to move on.

What do you look at for style inspiration?

Definitely 'Space 1999' and other GERRY ANDERSON television programmes. Also mid-to-late-'90s 'Star Trek'. I've always been obsessed with uniforms. My favourite book as a child was a magazine of USSR military uniforms and insignia. Around that time I wrote a letter to the German Polizei asking if they'd send me a uniform in child size: the olive drab blazer and khaki pants.

Can you describe the state of your closet? Is it tidy, messy, super organised?

My clothes live on a Scandinavian drying rack; I don't put them away. They're either on me, in the wash or drying at any given time.

Is there a garment that you used to dislike but ended up loving and wearing?

I don't usually wear colours, as I adhere to a strict black jeans and black T-shirt combination. But recently I've come into possession of a royal-blue Parisian street-cleaner's jacket, identical to the trademark garment of the late New York street-fashion photographer BILL CUNNINGHAM. I actually received it from my mum, who found four of the same jackets in a vintage shop and attempted to enforce a family uniform, to which I consented.

Have you ever been tempted to get rid of all your clothes and start again from scratch?

No. I've had the same clothes since I was about 14. I mostly wear VANS and I have no formal clothes. Weddings and funerals are definitely a panic.

Does your work influence what you wear?

I work for a (legally unnamable) technology company and I am usually allowed to dress casually for work. On occasion I am required to wear a coloured T-shirt, but I always insist on wearing a black long-sleeved T-shirt underneath, against my skin.

What do you wear to look sexy? Do you have a pick-up look?

No.

Can you share an amazing tip for wardrobe management or maintenance?

As aforementioned, a drying rack as a storage system. It has the added benefit of limiting your wardrobe to essentially a suitcase worth of clothes. Useful in case of sudden getaways.

What underwear do you wear?

I have never bought underwear. I am given it for Christmas. Most of it is plain black and from PRIMARK or similar.

What would you say ultimately signifies your style of dressing?

I look like a child who's just started dressing himself.

STEVEN GREGOR and the simple black T-shirt

A questionnaire from February 2017 with a 42-year-old editor and designer from London. Steven makes 'Gym Class' magazine, a publication about media.

What garment is key to your personal style?

A simple, black T-shirt.

How many black T-shirts do you have in your wardrobe?

About 15. I buy them in batches of five, always the same brand. I live in a very small flat in central London, so wardrobe space is scarce. I have a one-in, one-out policy.

What is it specifically about simple black T-shirts that you love?

Ease.

What are the defining specifications that make the perfect black T-shirt?

Durability. Most of my clothes are washed in hard water and dried in a dryer. It's tough on them.

How do you feel when you see other men wearing the same thing? Are you happy to have the whole world wear "your" garment or do you prefer to stand out?

Oh, I definitely do not like to stand out. I'm an all-black, head-to-toe kinda guy. I have no problem with other people dressing like me, but it would be a pretty boring world if everyone did. I love the theatre of fashion... I just don't want to perform in it. I prefer to dress like one of the ushers! However, I'd break my all-black rule for the burgundy-red "May the bridges I burn light the way" sweatshirt from VETEMENTS. I love it. Does it come in black?

Who or what do you typically look at for style inspiration?

Fashion magazines are still my main source of inspiration. Television and film are also an influence. I'm inspired by character and personality – personal style – more so than individual items of clothing.

Can you describe the state of your closet? Is it tidy, messy, super organised and are your

clothes folded, boxed, grouped by colour or season, etcetera?

Small is the best word to describe my closet. So, out of necessity, it's reasonably organised. I worked in a department store for a short time while at university. I was taught how to properly fold a T-shirt, fast. I don't own a washing machine, so all my clothes are laundered in a nearby launderette. The attendant who washes and folds my clothes is a star, but our methods differ greatly. It can be a little frustrating.

Is there a garment that you used to dislike but ended up loving and wearing? When did your aversion to it turn to fondness? What changed your mind?

I can't think of garment I used to dislike but now love. However, I spent my university years wearing checked shirts, blue jeans and brown R.M.WILLIAMS boots. That's a look I have no interest in reinstating.

Have you ever made a radical change in your "look"?

When I was younger I would regularly change my look. I found myself through reinvention. Nowadays, I have little desire to mix it up or change my style. That said, I'm interested in wearing better quality clothes. I'd like my day-to-day wardrobe to be less disposable. I would like to develop my personal style that way.

Does your work influence what you wear?

My weekday and weekend looks are exactly the same. I would not – could not – work anywhere that required me to wear a suit and tie every day. Even for formal social occasions, I try to find options other than a suit and tie. I've read countless interviews with people endlessly saying how great they feel in a well-tailored suit... I'm happy for them, but it's really not for me.

What do you wear to look sexy? Do you have a pick-up look?

My pick-up look is the same as my drop-off look, really. But I like to be prepared should a special occasion pop up. I have dry-cleaned and pressed shirts and trousers – black, of course – hanging in my wardrobe for date nights.

What amazing tip for wardrobe management can you share?

Always hang your clothes on sturdy and appropriate hangers. And utilise space – shelving, hanging space (with a deep enough drop) and a shoe rack are especially important in small spaces. Oh...and never, ever hoard. If you don't wear it, give it to charity, recycle it or throw it away.

JOE SCOTLAND and the Nike shorts

A questionnaire from December 2018 with the director of Studio Voltaire. Joe was interviewed in the headquarters of the arts charity, which at the time had been transformed into a temple.

What garment is key to your personal style?

It's kind of the wrong weather for it, but what I'm really into are quite short NIKE shorts. They've been an established part of my look for the past six or seven years.

How many do you have in your wardrobe?

I have about ten pairs.

Why did you start wearing them?

It was an attempt to be healthier – not just by wearing the shorts, but by actually using them and going to the gym. It didn't last that long, but the shorts did.

What are the defining specifications of the shorts? Are they running shorts, or football shorts, or just general purpose?

I actually don't know the technical terms. I think they are running shorts, but they aren't the super short ones, they aren't the ones with the slit.

The ones with a slit on the thigh are running shorts.

Right, I imagine they might be for football then... I mean, I really hate sports. The material is shiny, quite thin, they come up to about mid-thigh and they normally have this horrible netting, which I cut out.

Oh god, not netting. Maybe they are swimming shorts?

No, I don't think so. It's just meant to keep everything in place.

Netting is so horrible to wear.

Really uncomfortable. I remember a few times wearing them in the gym with the netting in, and it's just horrible.

What colour are your shorts, typically?

Black or dark blue. I experimented with a red pair and I didn't really like them. I felt my bum looked really big in them, and somehow black feels slimming. That's another reason why I really like the shorts. I feel very comfortable and confident with my legs and the shorts feel quite empowering. I continue wearing them until it gets really cold. It's only in the last few weeks that I've stopped wearing shorts.

And what have you transitioned into? What are you wearing on your legs today?

Boring trousers. They're from MARKS & SPENCER. They are really uncomfortable. I do this thing where I have loads of summer outfits and then the winter comes and I'm totally unprepared and reluctant to buy anything. So the other day I finally accepted I had to start wearing warmer clothes and I went into MARKS & SPENCER, just beause it was there. I think it was actually my first time ever buying clothes there.

Do you wear your shorts everywhere?

Everywhere. I like wearing them to benefactors' events with a smart shirt and shoes. I think there is something about having small shorts but then wearing large shirts; it's quite nice, that contrast.

Are the shorts covered up?

You might get a hint, or an inch. It might look like you are just in your boxer shorts. It suddenly becomes quite shocking. I've not tried shorts with a coat yet, but that might be similar.

Do your shorts have pockets? Some sports shorts don't have them.

Some do, and some don't. The no-pocket thing is really annoying. I've had to put my phone in my sock before.

Is there anything you dislike wearing?

Shorts aside, I tend not to have any black in my wardrobe. I think navy blue is the closest I get. I really hate black; I find it really boring. In the art world everyone wears black and I really hate it. I just find it uncomfortable to wear.

Do you generally feel uncomfortable in conservative clothing?

To an extent, but I also wear a lot of RALPH LAUREN. I quite like the weird, awful preppiness of it.

Have you ever changed your look radically?

I've always worn quite bright colours. In primary school I would always refuse to wear my uniform; my favourite outfit was a pair of bottle-green corduroys and a reversible red sweatshirt with a MICKEY MOUSE print on both sides. But then I had a weird phase when I was about 12 or 13, where I started getting men's magazines, but awful ones like 'FHM' or 'GQ'. I started trying to emulate what I'd seen in there, which was quite formal. I remember going to a charity shop and buying this disgusting waistcoat because I'd seen one in 'GQ'. It was very odd, but I was growing up in Bexhill-on-Sea in a pre-internet age, and that was a first glimpse into the wider world at a time when all I wanted was to get out of this shit seaside town. Then a couple of years later I discovered 'i-D' and my look totally changed.

Do you talk to men about clothes?

I talk to my boyfriend about clothes. He's much younger than me – I'm maybe twice his age – so it's quite fun, the stuff that he's into... some really hideous stuff.

Like what?

These gothy platform boots with studs. He's really into squat parties and gabber. I'm not really into gabber myself. I hated it in the '90s; I'm not going to like it now.

Oh wow. Does he wear those amazing baggy trousers with all the straps?

I think he showed me a pair once. It's quite interesting as he is young and his style is transitioning. I think he is the only man I talk to about clothes, which is odd as I would certainly talk to female friends about clothes. I'm quite surprised at that, actually. I've never thought about it. Why do I feel I can't talk to other men about clothes? You'd think a forward-thinking homosexual would be a bit more progressive about things like that.

BARRY LINNEN and his cycling-style top

A questionnaire from May 2018 with a Scottish-born hair colourist. Barry is the director of On the Floor London, his fabulous east London hair establishment.

What garment is key to your personal style?

It's a cycling-style top by COMME DES GARÇONS with the Pink Panther cartoon character on it.

How many examples of these cycling-style tops do you have in your wardrobe?

One.

Do you know where your attachment to this garment comes from? Is it something from your youth, or something you picked up from a specific person? When, who?

I've been obsessed with it for years. Years and years and years. I think I first saw it in an issue of 'i-D' when I was still living in Dundee. ALASDAIR McLELLAN shot it. It was typical ALASDAIR: handsome northern boys in amazing clothes. I'm not sure which issue, but the T-shirt has 2005 written on the back so there's a clue. Anyway, the Christmas before last, my housemate JOHN bought it for me as a present. It was an amazing gift.

What is it specifically about this garment that you love?

Partly because of the memory of that image and having been so obsessed with it for so long, partly because it's quite rare. But also because of the cycling-style cut. That's a big part of my look. I wear a lot of cycling tops.

Do you cycle?

I don't, no! I don't watch cycling; I couldn't tell you anything about it. I don't even own a bike. I just love the cut of cycling tops. I love their tight, high necks and that they usually come in really bright colours. I layer clothes a lot, and having a brightly coloured neck peeking out the top of something is a look I really like. I've got one other "fashion" cycling top, which is by WALTER VAN BEIRENDONCK, but I can't really wear it because it's too out there. It's really bright, luminously bright, and it says, "Do not eat the crocodiles," on the back of it. Then the rest of my cycling tops are a mixture of vintage ones that are made of wool and newer ones that are usually made of sporty Lycra stuff. My COMME top is made of Lycra.

Are you particularly fond of the COMME top because it's got lots of pink on it?

Hmmm. Not particularly. I do like pink, but I'm not really obsessed with it.

For the benefit of the reader it should be pointed out that we are in your salon, which is painted almost entirely pink, and you're wearing a pink shirt.

Ha! I realise how ridiculous it sounds, me saying that, standing in this room, but honestly, I'm more a fan of the cut than the colour. I'm just obsessed with necks. I like to feel really neat. I like my T-shirts to be really tight. If I'm wearing a shirt, my top button is always done up. I don't know if it's because I'm quite skinny, but I don't like too much of my neck area being on show. I sometimes struggle in the summer with just wearing a T-shirt. That makes me feel a bit weird.

Can you describe the state of your closet? Is it tidy, messy, super organised?

My bedroom literally just fits a double bed, and that's it. My wardrobe is out on the landing. It's a bit awkward at times but I quite like it. I always ask people's opinion of things, so it kind of suits me. I'll be looking through my wardrobe and grab anyone that's around and ask them what they think.

Have you ever made a radical change to your look?

There are things I used to wear that I'd probably never wear now. Like, I used to be obsessed with looking like a proper '80s skinhead rent boy. I've always had an obsession with '80s dressing, actually. I was still a little boy then, so it's me kind of revisiting the styles of the time that I wouldn't have been able to wear and getting a chance to wear them. Like JIMMY SOMERVILLE: faded denim, white T-shirts, green army jackets.

Do you have a dress code for work? Does cutting hair influence what you wear?

Not really. I can be very free with how I dress, and I love that.

You don't wear a little utility pack with all your kit in it? Or those comfortable clogs that chefs wear to protect the feet from sharp things?

Oh no! Because I'm in my own shop I've got all my stuff within reach. I don't need to carry it. And I just wear any old shoes. The ones I've got on right now are... This is a bit embarrassing. They are really, really shit plimsolls that I picked up from Brick Lane Market and I spray-painted the toe caps and soles. I'm quite DIY with my clothes. I like to bleach my clothes, too.

What do you wear to look sexy? Do you have a pick-up look?

Good socks. I've got these particularly nice WALTER socks. If it's the summer and you've got a good pair of shorts, some fresh white trainers, and a pair of fun WALTER socks:.. I would feel quite hot walking through London Fields with that on.

I've never thought of socks as being sexy, but I can see it.

My logic is this: if you're wearing good socks then guys will be looking at your legs. But, having said that, I can't confirm if anyone's ever actually tried to pick me up because of my socks.

FERNANDO AUGUSTO PACHECO and his short shorts

A questionnaire from June 2017 with a Brazilian radio journalist in London. Fernando makes and lends his voice to The Stack, Monocle 24's weekly show about print media.

What garment is key to your personal style?

Shorts.

How many pairs of shorts do you have in your wardrobe?

I have about 15 pairs of shorts.

What is it about shorts that you love?

I tend to dress better in the summer and shorts are essential for the season.

What are the defining specifications that make the perfect shorts?

For a more relaxed environment, I've recently started to enjoy larger, baggy shorts, which can be quite sexy. But people know me for my short shorts, like the RAF SIMONS and J.CREW five or seven inches. I still like them very much.

Are you happy to have the whole world wear "your" shorts or do you prefer to stand out?

To be honest, I would probably prefer to stand out rather than blend in.

Do you know where your attachment to shorts comes from?

It is not from my youth; I used to dress more conservatively when I was a kid. I liked wearing long sleeves, even in the summer. Shorts are a habit that I started after I turned 18. It was a means of liberation, I think.

What do you look at for style inspiration?

Fantastic Man is one of them for sure. Also, some workers from specific fields, such as builders, and old videoclips like 'Domino Dancing' by the PET SHOP BOYS.

Can you describe the state of your closet? Is it tidy, messy, super organised and are your clothes folded, boxed, grouped by colour or season, etcetera?

I'm not overly happy with the closet in my flat; it is not as organised as I want. Trousers and jackets are all together. T-shirts and polos are divided into everyday, work, sport, tropical ones and long-sleeved ones. I have recently become obsessed by how clothes smell. I spray something from THE WHITE COMPANY on them almost every day.

Is there a garment that you used to dislike but ended up loving and wearing?

I used to hate sportswear, as I was never a fan of the gym, but I recently bought some nice pieces from NIKE and LULULEMON and I like the way they fit. It makes going to the personal trainer more enjoyable.

Have you ever considered settling on a strict uniform and if so, what would it be? Would you consider it a relief, or a loss of options?

I wouldn't like to be one of those people who only wears one type of T-shirt or trousers. That would really stress me out. I would be very, very unhappy. However, I do wear certain things more often and my average look consists of ACNE jeans (I've been loving their black jeans recently), a slim fitting polo (usually by RALPH LAUREN), plus my trusted LEVI'S denim jacket and TIMBERLAND boots (although I'm considering buying CHURCH'S Chelsea boots for a change).

What would you say ultimately signifies your style of dressing?

I tend to compare people with animals. When I dress I like to imagine myself as an antelope with touches of macaw.

ANDREW BUNNEY and his search for the perfect white T-shirt

A questionnaire from July 2018 with the designer and creator of fine jewellery. Andrew loves to travel, more often than not to promote his label Bunney.

What garment is key to your personal style?

It would have to be the white T-shirt.

How many white T-shirts do you have in your wardrobe?

Upwards of 50 or 60.

Wow. That is a lot!

Yeah it is. I suppose I have two kinds really: ones for wearing as outerwear and ones that I wear under other garments. Once you have washed them a few times, no matter how clever or vigorous your washing routine, they lose their lustre and shape and become different things entirely from the ones you bought. I tend not to get rid of clothes.

Are they all from the same brand?

I'd love to say there is a specific brand I stick to, and I would stick to one if only I could. I have to hop around a lot because brands are always changing the details; you really like one and then after two years they change something. I am always looking for the "best in field", and I don't discriminate over brands. The kind I prefer at the moment are the Supima cotton ones from BROOKS BROTHERS.

What is it that you love so much about the white T-shirt?

It's quite classic, it's versatile and it's utilitarian. I think I always have one on.

Even if you weren't going to see it? Say, if you were wearing a shirt buttoned all the way up to the top?

Yeah, I think I would. Unless it were an extremely formal occasion...although I am not often invited to those.

What are the defining specifications that make the perfect white T-shirt?

The very specifics?

If you wouldn't mind.

For me, they are always plain, always crew-necked and always short-sleeved, but within that there is a whole range of differences. The neck is the most important part: for my outer T-shirts I prefer a beefier collar with a cover-stitch around it, but for my undergarments I don't like the cover-stitch. Now, this is getting really specific, but American-made T-shirts tend to last longer, as they have to cope with their top-loading washing machines, which are much more aggressive. Our European front-loaders are much kinder, which means our T-shirts don't need to be quite so strong. Shape-wise, it needs to be a little longer, and I don't want it to be boxy... Slim and long is the way to go.

How do you feel when you see other men wearing the same thing? Are you happy to have the whole world wear "your" garment or do you prefer to stand out?

Whilst I don't know if I could call myself an expert on the topic, I am certainly a connoisseur, and I love to see the differences between white T-shirts in other cities and other countries. It is such a pervasive wardrobe staple, but it is different all over the world. In Singapore and Hong Kong, for example, it is a very different cut; it looks much more formal and often won't have a ribbed collar. When I see someone wearing a nice white T-shirt I'm always curious as to where they got theirs from.

Is there a garment that you used to dislike but ended up loving and wearing? When did your aversion to it turn to fondness? What changed your mind?

As I get older I am less interested in making firm judgements about what is right and wrong. Of course I have my opinions, but I have been through enough cycles of fashion that I generally try and be open to things. There are certainly things I have worn at certain points in my life that would feel very foreign to wear now, but nothing that I would really classify as hating.

SAM McKNIGHT and the Fred Perry polo shirt

A questionnaire from February 2017 with the 61-year-old hair stylist. Sam was interviewed on the occasion of the exhibition 'Hair by Sam McKnight' at Somerset House, London.

What garment is key to your personal style?

My FRED PERRY polo shirts.

How many of these shirts do you have in your wardrobe?

At least 100. There's rarely a day that I don't wear one.

What is it about them that you love?

They are so simple and the colour combinations are great. The bad thing about them is that they shrink. Unfortunately, shrinkage and me are not compatible.

What are the defining specifications that make the perfect FRED PERRY polo shirt?

I specifically like their classic polos – no capsule collections or diffusions – although, I did love the COMME DES GARÇONS collaboration they did.

Do you know where your attachment to FRED PERRY comes from? Is it something from your youth, or something you picked up from a specific person? When, who?

It was actually through the COMME DES GARÇONS collection. I used to wear lots and lots of COMME but there comes a point in a man's life when crazy avant-garde pieces just don't work anymore. So this collection was a sort of gateway. I bought it because of how much I loved COMME and came out a FRED PERRY obsessive.

Who or what do you look at for style inspiration? Do you look at fashion?

I really don't look at anyone in particular. Not when it comes to my shirts. That said, I used to be an absolute fashion victim when I was younger. I had a particular thing for Japanese brands and I still have all my original COMME and YOHJI YAMAMOTO stuff from the early '80s. Lots of loose silhouettes with big shoulders. I have a lot of GAULTIER, and so many amazing pieces that VIVIENNE WESTWOOD made for me. This was before she was doing men's and she would make clothes for me out of her women's fabrics. I've got all sorts of things like double-breasted leopard-print suits and rose-embroidered wool trousers.

Can you describe the state of your closet? Is it tidy, messy, super organised?

I've just had some custom wardrobes built, which are great. They are very, very tall with a beech-veneer interior. Everything inside is well organised. I like everything colour-coded. All my FRED PERRY's are in one place. All my trousers are somewhere else, sorted by colour. Otherwise, I can't start my day properly.

What amazing tip for wardrobe management can you share?

Cedar balls. I put them in the drawers for moths. I also buy these smelly wax pomanders from SANTA MARIA NOVELLA that hang in the wardrobe. They give everything a nice air and counteract the mustiness of a moth buster.

Have you ever considered settling on a strict uniform and if so, what would it be? Would you consider it a relief, or a loss of options?

I had a school uniform when I was a kid and I loved it. I was proud of it. It was a deep maroon with a yellow trim. Very beautiful, I thought. Then after that I had one that was equally striking, which was navy blue and silver. In my later years the colour black became something of a uniform for me and it's something I am trying to break free from. I am on a mission not to wear black.

Do you have a dress code for work? Does your work influence what you wear?

I live in trainers. I do love my TRICKER'S brogues. However, I'm on my feet so much that I can't wear shoes regularly any more. Other than that, I just wear plain chinos from BANANA REPUBLIC or GAP. Hair styling can be a messy job, so I wear things I can just chuck in the washing machine afterwards. Deep pockets are very useful, too, as I don't like fancy tool belts. I just carry everything in my pocket.

Have you ever made a radical change in your "look"?

I did bleach my hair once, in 1985. I knew my hair was about to disappear, so I decided to have one last stand and had six glorious months as a blonde.

JONATHAN AMES and the sport coat

A questionnaire from August 2018 with the acclaimed American novelist. Jonathan was interviewed over the phone in his Los Angeles bedroom.

What garment is key to your personal style?

The sport coat is essential to my life and being out in the world. I don't know if you guys call it a sport coat in England. A sport coat could also be called a blazer, as in a blue blazer. But I'm not necessarily talking about the blue blazer. I'm talking about a jacket that is, you know, like the top of a suit but without matching pants. The BROOKS BROTHERS sport coat is the essential garment for me.

How many sport coats would you say you have in your wardrobe?

Let me open my closet... I have one, two, three, four, five. Four of them are from BROOKS BROTHERS. These days I'm mostly just wearing the two lighter ones. I have a dark blue one that I will wear at night to more formal, fancy things. I need new sport coats. I used to have a whole quiver, like an artist with a palette, but I don't have that many now. I used to probably have ten to twelve sport coats in New York and then I moved to Los Angeles, and my supplies completely winnowed. (continued on p. 70)

Live from PAUL SMITH's wardrobe

The designer who started selling from a tiny store in Nottingham nearly half a century ago marched on to become one of Britain's biggest and most recognisable fashion names. Paul Smith – or Sir Paul Smith, since 2000 – is the totally charming purveyor of twisted classicism who prefers to keep his clothes in their own bedroom. Unsurprisingly, he takes great precision and care in getting dressed at the start of each invariably busy day and likes to plan his outfits well in advance. Interview by PENNY MARTIN.

What is the first thing you do when you wake up?

I creep down to the jetlag room at quarter to, ten to six. It was named that years ago because I was travelling so much that I was always jetlagged and disturbing my wife, PAULINE, in the night. So it's a separate bedroom downstairs where I keep all my clothes and notebooks.

What else is in there?

There's a radio, and besides the rail for my suits, sock drawers and whatnot, I've got one of those valet stands, like you see in hotels. It's a lovely old JACQUES ADNET one. He worked for HERMÈS. It's leather, stretched over a frame and stitched.

Do you use it?

Oh yeah, I've normally got my clothes ready the night before, since someone will have told me what I'm doing the next day – I'm being photographed in an hour's time, for example, or I might be riding my bike.

Do you spend long deliberating on what to wear?

To be honest, it's nearly always a suit. So last night I was late – not late-late, midnight – but I still put this one out, ready, because I knew I was seeing you.

Describe it for me.

At the moment I tend to wear single-breasted, two-button suits with a relatively narrow lapel but a high notch – an Italian notch. On an Italian suit, that notch would be even higher, and the lapel would be much wider. But this is more of a British cut, like a HUNTSMAN or another Savile Row tailor that cuts slim. HUNTSMAN always cut slim because they have a strong link with the military; their customers were used to ceremonial dress, which was cut very slim.

How did you decide that was the cut for you?

Well, I'm tall. 181 centimetres, I think. I'm not that slim anymore.

Oh, come on, Sir PAUL, you're match fit!

My father was similar, and my brother was similar, so we've always worn what I suppose you would call "lean-looking suits". This one is in a very lightweight LORO PIANA fabric, which is very dark navy blue with a, what, 3-inch check. It was developed specially for PAUL SMITH – that's the company, not me – with a bouclé yarn, which gives a bit of texture, just makes it a touch more unusual.

A designer friend once told me you're the only other designer she ever sees at the Première Vision fabric fair.

I used to design fabrics in the mid '70s. I worked in Yorkshire for LEIGH MILLS, which is how I got my head around how to use yarn, or the difference between a compact weave and a loose weave. I've got this thing called a linen prover, which is a funny little magnifying glass measuring about a centimetre-squared. You put it onto fabric and look through it to see how tightly woven or loose it is. And not just that, you can also see how tightly spun the yarn is. Geeky, I know!

Are there fabrics that you would never wear?

We don't really make or use heavy fabrics like we used to – those of 14 and 18 ounces. Now, the average weight of fabric is more like eight to ten; the one I'm wearing is eight. The modern, lighter fabrics perform better, and with air conditioning, heated cars and public transport, a heavier weight isn't necessary. When I started designing in the '70s, a key reason for wearing a jacket was to keep you warm, not just to look good.

So no 14-ouncers in your wardrobe?

I have one – green-checked – which is 14-ounce, but with a softer handle. You can only wear these at certain times of the year, though, because they do feel heavy.

How many suits do you have on rotation?

There are 15 suits on the rail. Any more and PAULINE would tell me there was no room, that I'd have to give them away. It's quite a restricted space. I'm very organised, I suppose, but it's because I'm quite limited, intentionally.

Where do the excess suits go?

The archive in Nottingham. Back before that was operational, I had some amazing 100 per cent cashmere suits and some high-twist worsted suits that I took down to Portobello Road. I asked this young girl who had a stall there whether she'd like them, and she said, "No, sorry, I can't sell suits."

Not even from PAUL SMITH?

I didn't dare mention they were PAUL SMITH – too pretentious.

Is there a mirror in your wardrobe?

Just outside, beside the valet stand, with two lights either side. That's really important, to have light facing you rather than above you.

Why?

If it's above you, you look 108 years old. We've learned that from shop design. Years ago, I hadn't taken enough clothes with me on holiday and I went to buy a shirt from a shop where the light was positioned above me. It just looked terrible. I thought, "Never again are we doing a changing room like that." We have 16 architects and designers, in-house, who design all our shops. We've developed a type of mirror whose sides change to frosted glass with fluorescent lights behind it that shine straight onto you.

Friendly.

Yeah, you look gorgeous. Actually, one of the best places for that is in the bathrooms of Le Bristol hotel in Paris. You stand in front of that mirror and think, "Oh my God, I look amazing!"

Is it rare for you to buy another designer's clothes?

Over the years I've worn bits and bobs of COMME DES GARÇONS, because I'm very privileged to have been given them by REI. There are lots of things COMME do that I don't understand, but when they do a simple shirt, it's great. When I first opened my shop in the 1970s, we only had a few things with the PAUL SMITH label, because they had to be handmade by PAULINE or myself. So we also sold a bit of MARGARET HOWELL. I love MARGARET.

In what order do you get dressed?

I put my pants on first. I swim every day and find it really amusing to see people standing in the changing rooms, wearing their socks and nothing else. Especially if you have a fat belly. So, pants first, just to cover up, I suppose.

Are you particular about underwear?

If I'm wearing lighter trousers, which I have been for quite a while, then it's pretty hard wearing the boxer shorts, that I love, underneath.

Too much volume?

I far prefer a boxer short; I look dreadful in those skimpy pants.

Does the same go for your swimwear – a baggy, colourful short?

Yeah, I have a baggy black pair – either PAUL SMITH or SPEEDO. Black or navy. On holiday, I'll wear patterned ones.

What follows pants?

Socks. I get through a lot of socks. I often wear silly socks, but mainly they're dark navy and short – not the longer, Italian ones. And I like them chunky; that works with the plain-cap shoes I prefer, which are substantial. They wouldn't go with a fine sock.

What's a plain cap shoe? Lace-up, like an Oxford?

Well, these are made from horse. These ones I've got on are Cordovan Spanish leather and they're 32 years old.

Do you have a last?

I do. It was hand carved in Northamptonshire, but we keep it in Tuscany because we make our shoes there now. I've got quite a slim foot, but because I wear a plain-cap and they open quite a bit at the front – they've a Gibson front – it works well. I've got some trainers, but I don't really wear them.

Do you wear a vest?

In winter I'll wear a T-shirt under my shirt, just a plain white one, which I'll buy anywhere. Ours are usually printed.

Who does a good white T-shirt?

It's really hard to find a good one.

Which specific qualities are you looking for?

Fine gauge and the highest neck possible, because you want it to be visible under the open neck of a shirt. The best I've found is from INTIMISSIMI. MUJI do a great one but it's too short for my height. It would be good on you.

In press clippings I notice you used to wear a tie in the 1980s, but now, not so much.

I did occasionally in the early '80s, when everyone would button the collar right up to the neck. But that was more part of a look, really. And I did wear one to Buck House.

This was in 2000, to collect your knighthood from the Queen?

Yes, so you had to wear a tie there.

Did your father wear a tie every day?

Yes. He passed away when he was 94 and he still wore a shirt, jacket and tie every day, even when he was in the house.

Would he have been mortified to have been seen without one?

I think he would, yeah. He was a bit upset when I stopped wearing ties in the early 1970s. I wore a tie to my dad's funeral and I said to the coffin, "You would be pleased, Dad. I've got one on." And then I cried, like I am now.

Did your father have his suits made bespoke?

They were made to measure, rather than bespoke. With made to measure, you really just adjust the length of the jacket from a basic block, the length of the trousers, the length of the sleeve. Obviously, bespoke requires taking many more measurements and is made to fit you perfectly.

Do you think it was through your father's clothes that you became interested in the suit specifically?

Without realising, I think it was maybe because my dad always looked very smart and because he had a very nice, easy-going personality. His example certainly helped me build my business in places like Japan, where nobody really spoke English yet we had to communicate somehow.

What did he do for work?

He was something called a credit draper, which doesn't really exist anymore. He used to sell stuff like clothes, sheets and towels to people at their homes. Not knocking on doors – they had something called a round. After the war, when people didn't have much money and clothing and drapery warehouses opened all over the country, ex-insurance men, which my dad was, would call their round, and people would say, "Yes, HAROLD, could you bring me some sheets next week." And he would go to the warehouse and on sale-or-return bring three types of sheets or two types of jumper and you would say yes or no. He had a book in which he'd write down the order and you'd pay £2 a week and slowly buy the product.

That must have required a lot of discretion and kindness, visiting hard-up people in their homes.

I think my father was probably like a psychiatrist to a couple of hundred people. You see this watch? Let me take it off and show you the back. It's a homage to my dad. He was an amateur photographer; he built his own darkroom in the attic of the house. When I was 11, he bought me a camera and then I used to spend every Thursday in the darkroom with him, developing film and printing with the enlarger. We always used to have the red light on in the darkroom, so the red back of the watch is my homage to him.

Have you always worn a watch with hands, rather than a digital one?

Yes, and I need to wear one of ours. Sod's Law that if I wore someone else's, I'd be photographed in it and the press people would be banging their heads off the table. We sell about 90,000 watches a year.

But no other jewellery. No wedding ring?

Nope. But I've always liked these thread bracelets I have on. They're from India; I've worked with embroiderers and people that do things by hand there for a long time.

When you think of a suit, you think plain, classic, but you've actually found a lot of avenues for embellishment.

The PAUL SMITH way is that dreaded, overused expression: "classic with a twist." It's about irreverence or opposites, like my 32-year-old shoes or this belt... [Stands up, unbuckles and removes his belt] It's something like 15 or 20 years old and proper saddle leather. What I like is taking modern suits, good-quality suits, and putting them with a worn-in belt or a shirt that's frayed. The shirt I wore to my wedding was an old one.

When were you married?

In 2000. Same day as the knighthood. I mean, saying this is probably not very good for business, but for me personally, the suit itself is just something I wear. I think of it as a picture, as a frame.

What do you mean?

I'm a busy man. I literally have a meeting every hour of every day. I'm often going to Hong Kong for the day, to Vietnam for the day. So the half-canvas suits that I wear have to perform; they're a bit of kit. For CECIL BEATON and OSCAR WILDE and the BUNNY ROGERS of the world – all those famous dandies – the suit was something expressive. I love that, but personally, I don't have that luxury.

Are there things you wouldn't wear, now you're 72?

Not at all, because I'm not that extreme. If I were a red-suit man or a big-flowery-shirt man, then yes. I mean, I probably dressed in flowery shirts when I was 18 to 26, with long hair and too many scarves, pretending I was JIMI HENDRIX. But that was just a period of growing up. The first proper brush I had with tailoring was in 1966, with a tailor in Nottingham called Mr. HARRIS. I'd always been in love with a company called HUNT & WINTERBOTHAM. They were a merchant in Golden Square who did this amazing gaberdine fabric in a huge range of colours. I bought three and a half metres of mint-green and three and a half metres of dusty-pink and got Mr. HARRIS to make me a single-breasted suit in the pink and a double-breasted in the green. Wow. I must have looked ridiculous.

Is that part of you now in the colourful details – the handkerchief, the silly sock?

I guess so. Then the other part of my wardrobe is to do with a denim jacket, a lightweight cotton jacket, an old French railwaymen's jacket.

When would you wear those, if you're wearing a suit every day?

Very rarely, is the answer. Almost never. In the summer, if I'm away on holiday, I would probably wear the linen or cotton one, because I still like a jacket. I like pockets for my notebook, pens. I always carry some notepads plus two pens and a SHARPIE.

For autographs?

That is true, actually. And then the credit cards and the phone.

You must wear through your pocket linings with that lot in there.

I do, yeah. See this jacket here? It's completely knackered, but I love it. And then at the other end of the scale, I've got two or three beautiful overcoats, one of which is about 25 years old. It's amazing. It was made by our bespoke department in Westbourne House, and it's from the same 1000-gram wool as worn by the men who stand outside Buckingham Palace.

When would you wear that – for formal occasions?

Just on a really cold day. Formal is the way you dress things, the way you wear them, not necessarily the thing itself.

If you were invited to something that stipulated "black tie", what would you wear?

I would wear a black suit with a satin revere.

Is that a tuxedo?

A tuxedo would probably be in a barathea fabric, which is a very slightly twisted and woven fabric with a substantial weight, so it hangs beautifully. You can spend the whole night at a dinner and still look fantastic at the end of it.

You must be called upon to attend countless industry events.

I never go, though. PAULINE and I like to be on our own. We love each other.

Didn't she study couture at the Royal College of Art?

Yes, under JOANNE BROGDEN and JANEY IRONSIDE: icons of the industry. So PAULINE knew how to construct clothes properly, with pad stitching and what's called a *demette* – the sausage you put in at the shoulder. You know, I'd studied Palladian architecture when I was 21, but PAULINE could apply its laws of symmetry, its rhythm, to a jacket: window, window; pocket, pocket; portico, portico, portico.

What did you wear on your first date to impress her?

A suit, I'd imagine. It was my 21st birthday and I was very close to the art school in Nottingham. My dad gave me £21, so I spent it on drink and invited all the art students. PAULINE taught there two days a week then; she would travel up from London, where she was also designing for FOALE & TUFFIN. So it wasn't exactly a date that night. But it became a date later.

Does PAULINE tell you what she thinks you look handsome in?

She said I looked nice two nights ago when we went out for supper. I was wearing a checked suit – it's jade green, with these shoes and a similar coloured shirt. That's the great thing, the cheat about the way I dress: you look sort of slim and elegant because the suit is like a picture frame around you,

(Ends)

(continued from p. 63) **What is it specifically about the sport coat that you love?**

Some of it is fashion but a lot of it is utility: I have always seen the sport coat as the male purse. I have my wallet in the inside pocket near... What side is the heart on?

The left.

So, in the inside left pocket the wallet's there, close to the heart, although money is not important in that way. In the other pocket, by the right breast, I usually have a notepad of some kind with a pen, and then in the front pockets are my keys and cellphone. Living in Los Angeles, I also often go out with some form of marijuana in my pocket, whether it's pre-rolled or loose in my pocket along with what is called a "one hitter", which is a little pipe that looks like a cigarette. In my New York days I also liked having a paperback novel stuffed into the pocket for when I was on the subway.

When did you first start wearing sport coats, can you remember? What was it that drew you to them?

It was the early '90s; in fact I could almost pinpoint it. I went to Italy with my first novel in 1990, and I was beginning to have notions that I wanted to dress like a young gentleman and I thought the sport coat was essential to that. The blue blazer was the essential garment because you could wear it everywhere at any time and always look proper. The book was very dirty and dark and full of prostitutes and gritty downtown New York, and I had changed, I showed up in Italy to promote it wearing a blazer and a bow tie and I think they were like, "Where's the guy that wrote this dark, gritty erotic novel?" So it began in the '90s and I really was obsessed with it for many years. I wanted to look exactly the way authors did in their author photos. And then, over time, it became more about function and the male purse.

How often do you get new ones?

The last time I went shopping was a year ago. I was going to the Cannes Film Festival because the film of my novel 'You Were Never Really Here' was showing and I desperately needed some new clothes.

I greatly enjoyed that film. I don't know what you thought of it?

I really liked it. I thought it was a great adaptation and LYNNE RAMSAY did a fantastic job, JOAQUIN PHOENIX was brilliant, the score... It was a great adaptation of my book and a great film on its own. But to go to Cannes I needed some clothing, so I went to BROOKS BROTHERS and bought a pair of jeans and two different nice trousers and a blazer. I've never been a heavy person, but I started putting on some weight around the middle and I went to a doctor, and he told me to stop eating bread. I stopped eating bread and I lost 18 pounds! I'm back to my original trim self, but now all that clothing that I bought at BROOKS BROTHERS doesn't really fit anymore.

Are your sport coats mostly the same? You mentioned navy and a tweed one.

They tend to all be in variations of navy. I do have one plaid sport coat which I used to wear quite a lot, but I've kind of lost confidence in it.

Do you know why?

I don't know, maybe I got a few odd reactions at a certain point. I'd worn it confidently for years but then I lost faith in it.

Oh no, it's awful when your confidence in a garment gets knocked.

Yeah and it's just sitting there in good shape, it doesn't smell, there are no holes. I should try and resuscitate it. It's been lying low for about a year now, just sitting there forgotten. It looks at me with sad eyes, "You used to wear me; we used to have a good time together. What happened?" If I put it on I'll probably find some money in the pocket. You've encouraged me. Next chance I get I'm going to wear it.

Do it! You never know, maybe the public opinion will have changed. You shouldn't always dress to public opinion anyway.

Right, but I think one or two women I was dating might have been like, "I don't think that looks good." So that's probably what soured things. They put the kibosh on it.

That's tricky. Are they still in the picture?

Good point. Regardless of whoever it was that said it... There's definitely nobody in the picture for me right now! The sport coat has outlasted them. I'm looking at it right now. It has lovely golden brown hues and all sorts of lines – it's a really charming jacket. I'm going to wear it one night very soon. I miss it so much. This interview has really been very helpful, thank you.

MATTHEW MAZZUCCA and the blue pants

A questionnaire from December 2017 with the creative director of Barneys New York. Matthew grew up just across the water from the famed retailer, in New Jersey.

What garment is key to your personal style?

My whole code is really blue pants, which I typically wear with plain, black T-shirts.

How many of these blue pants do you have in your wardrobe?

I mean, I can't even get into my closet these days. It's floor-to-ceiling and it's basically all blue pants and black T-shirts.

What is it specifically about this garment that you love?

My background is in set design and set building, so I like having something quite utilitarian that I can wear every day but that is also simple enough to look smart. Because of my job, I'm apt to be painting a wall or driving a truck somewhere then throw a jacket on and sit in a meeting or go somewhere fancy, because there's still a formality to the pants. They are very versatile. I used to wear jeans but then I realised that when you don't wear jeans people take you more seriously.

What are the defining specifications that make the perfect pair of blue pants?

I can blast through a pair of pants pretty quickly, so they have to have stretch to them, be reinforced, have a coating. Coating means a lot to me. It means they repel all the day-to-day crap that gets on them and they last longer. I usually get them in thick cotton. When I started working at Barneys I began buying more designer stuff and I learned the hard way that there's a fragility to some designers, but weirdly it's not the ones you might expect. It's usually the more rugged looking, up-and-coming designers with a workwear aesthetic whose clothes are more fragile, whereas a pair of PRADA or DRIES VAN NOTEN blue pants are super tough and can take the rigour of what I do. They're, like, really tough, luxury workwear that you still have to get dry-cleaned.

Do you know where your attachment to blue pants comes from? Is it something from your youth, or something you picked up from a specific person? When, who?

I'm from New Jersey and grew up in a suburban, blue-collar neighbourhood, so utilitarian clothing has always been my go-to and something I'm fascinated by. Like, me and my friends used to chase down the local UPS truck so we could get the employee uniform magazine and order clothes from it. I think the pants specifically are from my dad. He was in construction and I would go and work with him as a kid and I remember all the CARHARTT pants. There was a huge importance in how you represented yourself. It wasn't about gilding the lily and using clothes to give yourself status; your substance came from how well and how hard you worked. So I've always worn these functional things, but now it's not DICKIES pants and HANES T-shirts; it's a more luxurious version.

It's interesting that you're able to wear the same type of thing you wore when you were growing up in Jersey but in a more updated manner. Is that important to you?

It makes me feel grown up. After 20 years in New York, just the sheen on my pants makes me feel like I've graduated to adulthood.

You've made it!

I made it, I made it! I'm wearing a belt now, my pants have a luxury finish and my T-shirt doesn't have a million holes in it.

Who or what do you look at for style inspiration? Do you look at fashion?

I basically live in Barneys and I'm often there when nobody else is there. It's like being in the Natural History Museum when it's closed. You can go through and look at every single garment at your own pace. I try not to look at any labels, though, because it's funny how much labels influence what you pick up. I like ploughing through the racks without looking at labels and just seeing what catches my eye. You can find some really interesting things that you might never have picked up.

Is there a garment that you used to dislike but ended up loving and wearing? When did your aversion to it turn to fondness? What changed your mind?

I never really liked wearing suits but recently I got curious. It sounds a bit backwards but I've started wearing suits on the weekends because I never get a chance to wear them for work. It's actually really fun. Only now, later in life, have I realised that if you dress really smart you can get away with so much more! You can get into lots of trouble and really push the limits of rebellion without being penalised when you're in a suit. It's a bit of a social experiment because people really do treat you certain ways based on the way that you dress. It's like that thing everyone said when I was a kid, "If you go to court you wear a suit because the judge is going to think that you're a good kid."

What amazing tip for wardrobe management or maintenance can you share?

My favourite, favourite thing is a steamer. I travel everywhere with a steamer, which everyone finds ridiculous, but then I find myself also steaming my friends' clothes whenever we travel. Nobody thinks to bring one and it's the best thing in the world. Irons are super intimidating to me, and so time-consuming. I just remember my parents always being stuck behind endless piles of ironing. Steamers are so much quicker, and the cheaper the better. A $20 steamer? Sign me up!

JOS GIBSON and his denim jeans

A questionnaire from November 2016 with a 40-year-old male groomer. Jos lives in London with his partner, Micka.

What garment is key to your personal style?

Denim jeans – I'm an absolute obsessive! Most people will tell you that they never see me without a pair of jeans on and always with turn-ups. I have a real fondness for CARHARTT's carpenter jean. ALEXANDER McQUEEN once told me they are the perfect fit, and he was totally right. I also love a NUDIE 'Sharp Bengt' but they don't make them anymore.

How many pairs of denim jeans do you have in your wardrobe?

About six pairs, including an amazing high-waisted pair by CRAIG GREEN.

What are the defining specifications that make the perfect denim jeans?

It's all about the fit on the waist, the bum and the thigh. It has to be right. The quality of the denim is important too – I like 12oz ideally – but I focus on fit the most.

Do you know where your attachment to denim jeans comes from? Is it something from your youth, or something you picked up from a specific person?

I'm not really sure where it came from, but probably my youth. My look has evolved over time and it has become easier to get better, heavyweight denim.

What do you look at for style inspiration?

I always keep an eye out for well-dressed people in London and I usually get fixated on a total stranger and how they dress. It hasn't happened for a while, but when it does it usually defines a change in style.

Can you describe the state of your closet? Is it tidy, messy, super organised and are your clothes folded, boxed, grouped by colour or season, etcetera?

There's this amazing kit from IKEA that's like scaffolding. It changed my life! My partner, MICKA, and I made our own bespoke walk-in wardrobe.

Is there a garment that you used to dislike but ended up loving and wearing?

Yes, that's happened a few times. It's usually something that's a different proportion or colour to what I normally wear and I'll put it on by accident or see MICKA wearing it and suddenly I'm obsessed.

Have you ever made a radical change in your "look"? Have you ever been tempted to start again from scratch?

Definitely. It happens most often when I look back at photos and think, "Ugh!" I once had this terrible phase where I only wore black, white and red together. It was like ZARA meets Russian Constructivists.

Have you ever considered settling on a strict uniform and if so, what would it be?

Uniforms are quite interesting but I think they are kind of really boring too. I'm not sure I'm that much of a fan.

Do you have a dress code for work?

Not really. I'm super casual. I want to feel comfortable and I'll probably wear one really key seasonal item. I'm a big fan of CRAIG GREEN jackets; I have about seven of them.

What do you wear to look sexy? Do you have a pick-up look?

Boots! I love a classic RED WING or CHIPPEWA boot on a guy. I don't think trainers are sexy.

What amazing tip for wardrobe management or maintenance can you share?

Get someone to build you a shoe rack out of plywood, it changed my shoe storage forever. No more fiddling with those silly expanding shoe racks on wheels.

What underwear do you wear?

SUNSPEL underwear is the best.

ISAIAH BARR and his musical hats

A questionnaire from August 2018 with a saxophonist from New York. Isaiah is one of the founding members of the exciting jazz ensemble Onyx Collective.

What garment is key to your personal style?

Hats! I think if you look at pretty much any photo of me, you'll see me in a hat.

What kind of hats in particular?

Oh, so many dude. Recently I got a few leopard-print women's rain hats from a 99-cent store in LA. I also just bought five new KANGOL hats, they're all bucket hats, so I have a purple KANGOL, a white KANGOL, a black KANGOL, an orange KANGOL, and a blue one. I also recently bought a vintage COMME DES GARÇONS corduroy hat with an all-over tie-dye print...

Just how many hats do you own?

I think probably 50 to 75.

How did your hat obsession start?

It started as soon as I started playing music. I was just a young saxophonist, so I didn't really have my own style and was just emulating what other saxophonists did. I started wearing black fedoras, the kind of hats old Brooklyn jazz musicians would wear – my mentor, ROY NATHANSON, always wears a fedora. From there I started experimenting with hats as I started experimenting with my music. I think the hat is just an essential part of performing. And I think the beautiful thing about styles in music is that it allows you to embody a different style of dress – to channel a different part of who you are.

So your hats are connected to your music?

For sure. If I'm playing in an old-school jazz set in a gallery with my mentor, I'm not going to show up in a leopard-print hat. I might wear a vintage PERRY ELLIS paperboy hat that my mom gave me. It's more subtle, more humble. Or let's say I'm playing something more spiritual or a little wild, I will wear something baggier, more eastern looking. If I'm playing a funk set, it's got to be a wild, crazy hat. I have furry hats that I got in Tokyo, very BOOTSY COLLINS: huge hats that fill up your whole head and have a curved, furry brim.

Do you dress from the hat down?

I always start from the hat!

As you dress thinking about music, would you say you look at other musicians for style inspiration instead of fashion, or do you look at fashion as well?

I look at other musicians. Some people just create their own reference points and I definitely do, but I'm also rooted in studying things. I look at what BOOTSY COLLINS and SLY STONE wore or NEIL YOUNG in the late '60s, early '70s. Later era MILES DAVIS: he looked like an alien or a Martian.

Do you think your dress sense has changed over time? Or are you quite consistent?

I've always liked standing out, but now I'm even more open with it. I just went to the release show for our record and I had on a very long white paisley shirt with ruffles on the front, then these really baggy paisley pants from Japan and this interesting, new bucket hat, which is striped. I like bootleg things, too; I have a lot of fake VERSACE. I mean, I have designer stuff, too, but I actually appreciate a lot of the copies that you can get in Jamaica or Miami that are not like the super realistic fakes you find on Canal Street.

Because they come out a bit weird and interesting compared to an accurate knock-off?

Exactly, because they're not perfect, they have something different to them. It's, like, "Oh wow, that's an interesting design."

JOHN PAWSON and the white, white shirt

A questionnaire from November 2017 with the British architect. John was interviewed in the minimalist surroundings of his Kings Cross office while eating a salad.

What garment is key to your personal style?

It's difficult to beat a white, white shirt.

How many examples of those shirts do you have in your wardrobe?

I have very few things – probably a few white shirts along with a few pairs of chinos. I hang on to my shirts until they are literally ripping apart. I think it's from my mother; she had this thing where she thought that men with threadbare shirts were somehow honest. She loved patches on jackets.

What is it specifically about white, white shirts that you love?

They are such beautiful things to slip into, like white linen sheets. Also I just love the colour white; I could be an evangelist for it. I daydream about beautiful alabaster, or sea salt, or white sands in the sun, or Moroccan plasterwork that's slightly veiny like old porcelain. Obviously, white isn't technically a colour in itself, but it's so varied and it reflects colour. It picks up its surroundings – the green in the garden, for example. You just can't beat it.

Do you know where your attachment to this garment comes from? Is it something from your youth, or something you picked up from a specific person? When, who?

I remember when I was younger and spent time with the designer SHIRO KURAMATA in Japan, he would always have the most amazing starched white shirts. When you sent them to the cleaner there they would always get starched, unless you asked them not to, so they'd be absolutely rigid. They felt like cardboard but looked amazing.

Is it hard to keep white, white shirts clean?

To keep shirts as fresh and as white as possible I wash them on their own, not even with white socks or T-shirts. But I have learnt to never bother about stains or things spilling on me. I was in Marrakech with my wife, CATHERINE, at a restaurant. They brought the tagine out and the waiter dropped the lid straight into it and it just went, splooosh! Just like that, absolutely everywhere. Of course I was wearing white and it made this incredible pattern all over my shirt. Everyone there was looking at me and I didn't react. They were all amazed that I kept wearing it, but I quite liked the pattern. In general, I feel it's important not to care too much about material things.

Is there anything you can't stand getting stains on?

Funnily enough, one of the only places I really don't like getting stains on is my pullover. They're hard to see and they rarely look good; usually just like you've spilled a bit of messy food down yourself. Ties as well: you can't have a stained tie. They're so hard to dry-clean. But really, the key to stains is to not lose your head and not get upset. It's the same with losing things.

Do you lose things often?

From time to time. We went away to Spain recently for a long weekend. There was a change of plan and I couldn't go home to pack, so CATHERINE very kindly packed for me but she forgot my shirts. I had this one white shirt that got washed every morning, because in Spain it could be washed and dried in an instant. I just felt free.

Who or what do you look at for style inspiration? Do you look at fashion?

No, not really. CATHERINE buys most of my clothes for me. She tries to get me to wear blue shirts because they match my eyes but I obviously prefer white ones. Then I tend to wear grey trousers in the winter and khaki in summer. Most of my things are from RALPH LAUREN. I should make more of an effort, really. Shoes are a bit of an effort; they're hard to get for someone else, so I often get those for myself. I recently wore out my red trainers, so I went and bought myself a new pair of bright white ones; these are called "Pure White" by ASICS or something like that.

They've got some interesting stains on them.

I spilled red wine on them the day I got them. It was my son BEN's 27th birthday and I managed to get a big splash of red on them.

What are the green marks?

It's some sort of plant. I was deep in the undergrowth in Spain, you see, and I managed to get lots of bits of plant stuck into them. Can you see the thorns too? I got most of them out, but there are still a few in there. I'm going to hold on to these for a while, though, despite the stains. I find it such a pain getting new ones.

What amazing tip for wardrobe management or maintenance can you share?

Use white clothing in moderation. The all-white suit is not a good look; you end up looking like a dentist, or a sailor, or a steward on an airplane.

JÉRÉMIE EGRY and the oversized coat

A questionnaire from April 2017 with the Paris-based designer. Originally from Grenoble, France, Jérémie is the founder and creative director of Études.

What garment is key to your personal style?

An oversized coat.

How many oversized coats do you have in your wardrobe?

I have a few different ones from ÉTUDES. They range from grey to black, and from wool to nylon.

What is it specifically about oversized coats that you love?

The elegance of a masculine, sober, long, warm coat. It must have really large pockets, which can easily hold books, a phone, keys, a bottle of water – all at the same time.

What are the defining specifications that make the perfect coat?

The volume. I really appreciate the size of this kind of coat. The style looks right thanks to the shape and the weight of fabric. Also, the size of pockets makes it look bigger, stronger. I feel good in it, almost protected. I could go everywhere with this coat on. I could brave the world.

Do you look at fashion for inspiration?

I am not very attentive to what is fashionable, even if some of my work is a reflection on men's fashion today. I am more sensitive to what surrounds us, our society, our cities, our means of communication, experiences...

Have you ever considered settling on a strict uniform and if so, what would it be?

I think I can describe my daily look as a contemporary uniform, in a sense. Black Dr. MARTENS boots, black five-pocket jeans, a black T-shirt, a black LEVI'S denim jacket and a black oversized wool coat. I like the difference between these black shades, naturally created by the different fabrics. I like the idea of wearing timeless clothes, pieces that are still icons of some cultures or movement.

Can you describe the state of your closet? Is it tidy, messy, super organized and are your clothes folded, boxed, grouped by colour or season, etcetera?

Super messy. Since everything looks almost the same, especially in the morning, I just pick what's on the top of the pile.

HAYDEN THORPE and the work shirt

A questionnaire from January 2017 with the lead singer of Wild Beasts. Hayden was interviewed while on a tour bus in Belgium.

What garment is key to your personal style?

The work shirt.

How many work shirts would you say you have in your wardrobe?

About ten, five of which are black and look exactly the same. They are all variations on the theme of black and grey – very forgiving colours – and various thicknesses for different times of the year.

What is it specifically about these shirts that you love?

Through its sheer practicality, the work shirt has become the most vital part of my wardrobe. It is the Swiss army knife of clothing, with a compartment for everything I may need when going on tour. I wear them so often that they have become part of my persona. I may not be alone in this habit but I have a "Hayden uniform" that I have to wear for the job of being me. When I put a work shirt on I think, "Okay I'm ready to be me now. Let's get the day started." The only time I break from this is when I'm on stage, where I am currently wearing a cut-off denim waistcoat and matching jeans a la 'Born to Run'-era BRUCE SPRINGSTEEN.

What are the defining specifications that make the perfect work shirt?

It's all about the pockets. You want an inside secret pocket, two pockets on either side of the lower torso – ideally with a smaller pocket within those – then at least one chest pocket to top it off. You're usually looking at around four or five pockets minimum for a good work shirt. My favourite has six.

Do you know where your attachment to them comes from?

I think it's from my barber, growing up. He wore them and would keep untold numbers of bits and bobs stored in his pockets. He always looked so effortless and like he had his entire life sorted out. A life organised through a shirt.

How do you feel when you see other men wearing the same thing? Are you happy to have the whole world wear work shirts or do you prefer to stand out?

I definitely feel a bit threatened. I associate myself so strongly with work shirts, so it can be strange seeing them on another person. However, if I see one I really like I'll simply look on longingly. I saw a guy in London recently with a beautiful work shirt and I stared at it for so long that he came over to ask me what I wanted. I was too embarrassed to ask him about the shirt.

Who or what do you look at for style inspiration? Do you look at fashion?

I look at our road crew a lot. They have very tough jobs and wear clothes that are highly practical, which I like. I spend a lot of time looking at wholesale trade catalogues for industrial workwear. Big books full of things like highly durable DICKIES trousers and overalls that you can only buy en mass.

Can you describe the state of your closet? Is it tidy, messy, super organised and are your clothes folded, boxed, grouped by colour or season, etcetera?

My current wardrobe is immaculate, as I'm on tour. I did a big tidy-and-storage session and it feels like part of my life has been cryogenically frozen, awaiting my return.

Is there a garment that you used to dislike but ended up loving and wearing?

That happens to me quite often. In fact, the jeans I am wearing this very moment are a pair of LEVI'S I bought about two years ago and didn't really like. I hadn't worn them at all and then a couple of days before we left on tour I put them on and, lo and behold, they are exactly what I want in life. I've worn them almost every day for the last month. The denim is slightly elasticated, which I initially thought was weird, but now I am on tour buses and planes for prolonged periods of time that bit of extra give is perfect. Elastic is the traveller's friend.

Have you ever made a radical change in your "look"? Have you ever been tempted to get rid of all your clothes and start again from scratch?

No radical changes, but it has been a long and often ugly journey to get my wardrobe to the state it's in now. I have reached the happy balance where 90 per cent of the things I own are compatible and I don't have to think about what I am going to wear on any particular day. I remember when we first played South by Southwest in the States, I was wearing a huge wide-brimmed felt hat, a bandana and a tie-dyed shirt. It was a bit of a disaster.

What do you wear to look sexy? Do you have a pick-up look?

No. I think I just wear my uniform. My philosophy is: "This is me. Why should I want you to be attracted to anything other than who I am?"

What amazing tip for wardrobe management or maintenance can you share?

A good T-shirt fold is both space-saving and just a delight. Neatly folding a T-shirt brings me so much joy and I am still refining my technique.

MICKA AGOSTA and the lightweight jacket

A questionnaire from November 2016 with a costume designer. Micka has worked on a number of screen projects, including the popular Marvel film 'Guardians of the Galaxy'.

What garment is key to your personal style?

A lightweight jacket.

How many lightweight jackets do you have in your wardrobe?

Over 10, possibly 20 if you include shirt jackets and the odd kimono.

What is it specifically about lightweight jackets that you love?

I tend to layer my clothes. I'm also one of those people that leaves the house with too much on, but feel I need to be prepared for any weather condition, even if it's a light wind on a warm day.

Do you know where your attachment to them comes from?

I just think you can never have enough light jackets. As I said, I like to layer!

Are you happy to have the whole world wear "your" jackets or do you prefer to stand out?

I like to see myself wearing my clothes more than other people wearing them. I'm a bit of a collector, or hoarder (depends how you see it). I started young and it comes with my job: working with clothes for film and TV.

I do like my classics – bombers, macs, work coats – and especially so if they have been made with a twist. I've always loved finding unusually constructed items from a charity shop or a weird shop out in the middle of nowhere. Clothes are always the first impression that you will get of a person, or a character. I like my clothes to say who I am, or perhaps who I am on a particular day.

Who or what do you look at for style inspiration? Do you look at fashion?

I like a mix of old and new. I look at films, old photos and friends. I do look at fashion, but not directly at current fashion trends. I have a very broad mood board.

Is there a garment that you used to dislike but ended up loving and wearing? What changed your mind?

I tend to wear something until I get bored with it, and just before I go to throw it out, it's suddenly the most important item in my wardrobe. This cycle is vicious.

Have you ever considered settling on a strict uniform and if so, what would it be?

I once thought I could dress like PICASSO. In his later years he wore the same thing constantly: chinos, or chino shorts, and a Breton shirt. My attempt lasted a week.

What do you wear to look sexy?

Depends on the situation and the venue.

Who do you talk to when you want to talk about clothes?

I talk clothes all day: at work and home. I can't escape it!

What underwear do you wear?

With jeans or trousers, I've reverted to wearing boxers. J.CREW boxers are my favourite. When I wear shorts (which I often do even through winter), I wear briefs, because you don't want your mates to pop out unexpectedly. I'm talking from experience.

What amazing tip for wardrobe maintenance can you share?

If you buy something that is second-hand and made of natural fibre, make sure you bag it and put it in the freezer for a week. This kills any insect friends and helps reduce that dusty-old-man smell.

NICK WOOSTER and the blue oxford shirt

A questionnaire from October 2016 with the menswear expert. Nick is particularly well known for his exquisite dress sense, which has made him a bona fide social media superstar.

What garment is key to your personal style?

A blue oxford shirt is literally the thing that I've worn for 45 years.

How many blue oxford shirts do you have in your wardrobe?

Probably 50. I always say I don't need another blue shirt but then I see one and it's, like, "Oh, I need that one!" Which is the stupidest thing in the world.

What are the defining specifications that make the perfect blue oxford shirt?

The key to a buttoned-up collared shirt is the roll of the collar; it should have a natural soft roll and not stand up like cardboard. That's how you can tell the quality. That and the weight of the fabric: it should be sturdy cloth. And they don't have to be expensive, by the way. I mean, they can be if you buy one from THOM BROWNE. But at the end of the day, a simple shirt from BROOKS BROTHERS or J.CREW is perfect. They're like 70 bucks, or something.

Do you know where your attachment to blue oxford shirts comes from?

Forty years ago this year, I started working for a clothing store in Salina, Kansas called Joseph P. Roth & Sons Clothiers and it was the best clothing store in town. I'll never forget: the two brothers, who were the sons of the owner, always wore blue oxford shirts. I remember thinking, "What is that?" because they reminded me of my dad's chambray work shirts but more refined. Whenever I see a blue oxford shirt I still get that feeling. It just seems correct. And by that I mean it always looks good. These guys were handsome and I wanted to be like them. I was probably in love with one of them.

Would you say you have a fetish for blue oxford shirts?

Well, yes, they do kind of give me a little bit of a hard-on. I love them! They are the one thing absolutely everybody looks good in and they really are the solution for any guy's dressing dilemma.

How do you feel when you see other men wearing the same thing? Are you happy to have the whole world wear "your" blue shirt or do you prefer to stand out?

Yes, I am a huge fan of people copying or borrowing, in general. Not necessarily borrowing my actual clothes, but going out and buying the same pieces. I'm totally okay with that. At the end of the day, clothes never look the same on any two people.

Can you describe the state of your closet? Is it tidy, messy, super organised and are your clothes folded, boxed, grouped by colour or season, etcetera?

I'm very bipolar when it comes to my wardrobe. I can go from being super disciplined, super anal, super organised to being a complete mess, all in the same day, week, place, month – it's constant. I need to have everything generally organised and then I can make a mess within that organisation. So part of the deal with my housekeeper is that she knows how to organise things by colour, or like-by-like. All the slip-on tennis shoes go here, all the oxford shirts go here. It has to be organised and then I make a mess. And then she comes back the next week and fixes it.

Have you ever made a radical change in your look? Have you ever been tempted to get rid of all your clothes and start again from scratch?

Certainly. In the '90s, in the era of HELMUT LANG and the beginning of MARGIELA, I had a very minimal period. All of those brands, PRADA and CALVIN KLEIN included, were doing something deceptively simple that I was really into for a while.

Is there a garment that you used to dislike but ended up loving and wearing?

I have changed my mind about heather-grey T-shirts. I used to hate them because they seemed like such a gym thing, and wearing heather for anything other than sweating seemed wildly inappropriate. But now I've turned a corner and I think they are perfect and go with anything.

Have you ever been tempted to get rid of all your clothes and start again from scratch?

Never! I still have wingtip shoes that are 30 years old. I still have an alligator belt from RALPH LAUREN that's 25 years old. Not shirts, because I don't think those keep well, but I have tweed jackets... I have a suede jacket of my father's. Even if I don't wear them I like knowing that they're there. I still have the first designer overcoat that I bought from PERRY ELLIS in 1984. It looks terrible but it's such an amazing coat. A friend of mine is a costume designer for Broadway and it's been used in two productions. It's come and gone in different shows but I still have it.

Have you ever considered settling on a strict uniform and if so, what would it be? Would you consider it a relief, or a loss of options?

To me, a uniform is the absolute chicest thing in the world. I know that I've created a monster for myself with this whole thing of dressing up. But I've always been like this – I'm a bundle of insecurities. I look at people who have a uniform as the most secure people on the planet. And I wish I was one of them.

WHAT MEN WEAR

A Fantastic Man book by
Gert Jonkers, Jop van Bennekom,
Eliot Haworth, Helios Capdevila,
Elizabeth Sims, Antonia Webb
and Jamie MacRae

Edited by Eliot Haworth
and Gert Jonkers

Designed by Helios Capdevila
and Jop van Bennekom

Many thanks to Penny Martin,
Seb Emina, Megan Wray Schertler,
Mark Smith, Tom Johnston and
Browns, the London-based luxury
boutique who very kindly supported
this print publication

Printed by Die Keure, Belgium
First published in 2019

Supported by

Browns

brownsfashion.com

Fantastic Man's online series of
questionnaires continues on
fantasticman.com/questionnaire